ALBERT SCHWEITZER:

Genius in the Jungle

To my sister Helen

Albert Schweitzer:

Genius in the Jungle

BY JOSEPH GOLLOMB

AUTHOR OF "THAT YEAR AT LINCOLN HIGH," ETC.

THE VANGUARD PRESS, INC.

NEW YORK

Sixteenth Printing

Copyright, 1949, by The Vanguard Press, Inc.

Published simultaneously in Canada by the
Copp Clark Company, Ltd., Toronto

ACKNOWLEDGMENTS

For permission to quote, acknowledgment is due to The Mac-
millan Co., Henry Holt & Co., Harper & Bros., The Beacon Press,
and Dr. Emory Ross of the Albert Schweitzer Fellowship as follows:

From *On the Edge of the Primeval Forest, J. S. Bach, The Decay
and the Restoration of Civilization,* and *Memoirs of Childhood and
Youth,* all by Albert Schweitzer and all published by The Mac-
millan Co.

From *Prophet in the Wilderness* by Hermann Hagedorn. Copyright, 1947, by Hermann Hagedorn.

From *Out of My Life and Thought* by Albert Schweitzer. Copyright, 1933, 1949, by Henry Holt & Co., Inc.

From *Albert Schweitzer: The Man and His Mind* by George
Seaver. Copyright, 1947, by Harper & Bros.

From *Goethe: Two Addresses* by Albert Schweitzer, translated
by Charles R. Joy and C. T. Campion. Copyright, 1948, by The
Beacon Press.

From the article, *"A Sunday at Lambarene"* by Albert Schweitzer,
published in *The Christian Century.*

DESIGNED BY MARSHALL LEE

Manufactured in the United States of America by
H. Wolff, New York, N. Y.

part one

———

1

THE baby was born so puny and turned so sickly
that at one time they actually thought he had died.

But he hung on.

When he was six months old the family moved to a
nearby village, and to meet their new neighbors the
mother invited them to a party at her home. She dressed
the boy in a white frock and colored ribbons. The
guests could not tell how she really felt about him,
though obviously she was showing him off. Her emotion was always controlled, and even with her family
her manner was reserved. But when the party was over
she went up to her room, locked the door, and wept.

The guests had said polite things, but she could see in their faces what they thought of the prospects for the undersized, half-alive infant.

But he hung on.

And milk from their neighbor's excellent cow had helped. Bracing air from the pines and the hills around the village and from the mountains behind them made him hungry, and that helped. Now when he slept it was no longer from weakness. Every cell in his body grew greedy, and his bones, muscles, and frame sucked in nourishment and growth, more than making up for lost time.

His eyes awoke, great, gray-blue, and wide apart, the eyes of a newcomer who finds himself in astonishing surroundings. Then they, too, grew greedy to take it all in, as did all his other faculties, but most of all his feeling for sound. He cocked his head at everything he heard, often as if he were listening to music and did not want to miss a note.

His mother's face, when she was alone with him now, had lost its look of suspense, and sometimes she even smiled in secret.

By his second birthday he had outstripped in size and sturdiness the average youngster of his age.

With it all came character, remarkably early, or at least a sense of what is right and wrong for a sturdy boy. He was still wearing dresses one day when he was watching his father work at the beehive in their garden. The boy gazed with wonder at everything, but most wonderful of all was the tall, kind, serious man whom he had followed everywhere and imitated in every way he could.

The man seemed to have made friends with the buzzing little creatures about the hive, so when one of them lit on the boy's arm he, too, tried to be friendly. The next moment he let out a howl of pain.

People came running. A servant girl took him up in her arms. His mother reproached her husband for not keeping the boy away from the hive. A neighbor or two, women, joined the commotion over the boy. His father felt sorry and said so, but he was the only one who did not behave as though a major tragedy had taken place. But the women examined the boy's arm, catered to him, and kept it up till he began to feel important.

Then he noticed that the pain was subsiding. He knew that if he stopped crying he would lose the center of the stage, so he deliberately held it. Then he saw the expression on his father's face. It was still kind, but he looked puzzled. He seemed to be asking, "Is this my son who is keeping up such a fuss about a little pain?"

But there was no longer pain, and the boy had to make a choice. He could keep on crying and retain the attention of the women. Or he could stop and regain his father's respect.

He kept on crying.

But many years later Albert Schweitzer remembered how guilty and miserable he had felt all the rest of that day and long afterward. "How often this experience of mine," he wrote, "has warned me against making too much of whatever has happened to me."

Whenever Schweitzer felt guilty he did something about it, and at the age of two, after that one experience, he stopped being a crybaby and learned how to take pain—when it was his own. How he reacted toward pain in others, even of animals, has been quite a different story.

2

THE three-year-old felt safe and proud as he sat between his mother and their servant girl, whose hands in white cotton gloves were crossed primly in her lap. He felt proud partly because he was now old enough to be taken to church, and this was his first time in what seemed to him a vast and dazzlingly beautiful edifice.

But most of all he was proud because that was his

father who stood alone before that elevation on which there was such a bank of flowers, such magnificent silver candlesticks, and images so rich in color. Every eye in the church was on his father as he intoned something, and the people repeated after him softly, their voices partly glad and yet, it seemed to the boy, a little afraid, too.

At home he was accustomed to the gentle tones of the big, square piano when his father's fingers wandered over its keys at twilight. The loudest music the boy had ever heard was when he himself would strike the piano, his foot on one of the pedals. Now suddenly a terrifying music broke forth in the church gallery, as if great thunder had burst into song along with snarling silver trumpets and golden voices. It roared over him like a surf, sent a wonderful shuddering shock through him, stopped his breath, hurt his ears, and made his heart so pound with panic that he turned agonized eyes on his mother.

Her face was serene, her eyes on his father. Even the servant girl sat unmoved. In fact, nobody in the church seemed to be aware that anything out of the ordinary had happened.

But not for long. Suddenly they, too, were caught up in excitement and began to sing along with the music. Relieved now that he could give voice to his own emotion, the boy sang, too. He had not the least idea what he was singing, but he gave it ardor and lung power.

Albert Schweitzer

A hand in a cotton glove gently closed over his mouth.

Something told him—perhaps it was his acutely sensitive hearing—that he had been singing out of time and tune, and he stopped. But all the rest of him kept on singing.

For now that he had recovered his breath, what had been terrifying had turned into something stirringly beautiful, and he looked up to see what prodigious instrument could produce such music. He saw a pyramid of golden pipes in a slant of sunlight, and though he could not see the player he guessed that the instrument must have keys much like the piano at home.

A wild wish now seized the boy to press those keys himself, an urge so overpowering that he actually started to leave the pew, but he was stopped by the servant girl. She thought he was only restless.

Not many years later the boy's wish was realized beyond any wild dream he could have ever had. But on that first Sunday all he could do was devour the heavenly instrument with his eyes.

All of a sudden they became glazed with horror.

By the side of the golden pipes there was something that he had thought was a tiny window, though he could nor see through it, so brilliant was the sun in it. He had not paid much attention to it at first. Now he saw a shaggy face there, a beard and black eyes squinting stealthily down into the church, watching every movement of the boy's father. And were they horns that curled out of that hairy forehead?

Genius in the Jungle

They were. It was the Devil!

Jägle, who dug graves in the churchyard, had told the boy all about the Devil. There was a sturdy common sense in the youngster that had tried to resist the stories as too terrible to be true. Now he saw how wrong he was, and his heart was again pounding with panic.

At such a time you either run crying for help or you freeze with terror, imprisoned in it and alone with the Thing. The boy froze. From what Jägle had told him he was sure that even if he cried out and the whole church should turn to see, it would be too late for him and for them. For the Devil would snatch him off and blow up the church with a burst of hellfire. So the boy sat watching, waiting . . .

The music had stopped, and the boy's father now walked over to a small raised platform, partly enclosed, and, mounting it, began to speak. But he was not looking at the people in the church. His face was uplifted, and he was praying for blessing and protection for them all, addressing himself to someone called Our Father. For all his terror the boy knew it could not be Grandfather Schweitzer, but none of it would have mattered in the least to him, were it not for a blessed miracle that had taken place.

The moment the boy's father had appealed to *his* father, the face vanished. . . .

Breath returned tremulously to the boy, and though his heart still misbehaved, a great wave of relief came over him, and he leaned against his mother, wanting to

9

cry a little, but he must not bring disgrace upon his father by making the whole church turn to look. . . .

So that was it, was it? His father could drive the Devil off with just a word to that even mightier Father. . . .

But the three-year-old was in no condition to give the great discovery much thought. He was worn out with so much emotion in one day, and with a sigh of exhaustion his body grew heavy against his mother's side, his head drooped, and his eyes closed.

Again fingers closed gently over his mouth, to soften an audible yawn, but this time the hand was his mother's.

The Devil returned next Sunday, however, and many Sundays thereafter, but every time he reappeared it took only a word of prayer to drive him off.

It is no wonder that church became a poignant and recurrent drama for the boy—majestic music, stark fear alternating with relief as great, thanks to some awe-inspiring source.

With time the fear grew less and finally died. The relief remained, strengthened, and grew into an all-embracing faith.

The boy did not say anything about the Devil to a single soul for a long time. He was partly still afraid of what the Devil might do. Later he kept silent about it because the whole matter had been a profoundly private experience, and like his mother, the boy and then the man always kept his deepest concerns to himself.

He learned eventually that what he had thought was
a window by the side of the golden pipes was really
a mirror, and the face in it, far from being that of the
Devil, was only "Daddy" Iltis, the church organist,
who sat with his back to the services and had to look
in the mirror to see when to play.

"Daddy" Iltis became the boy's first organ teacher.

Even the Devil had served. For in later years Albert
Schweitzer wrote that those Sunday experiences with
him "gave my childhood religion a distinctive touch."

3

AMONG the statues in that great and glamorous
square in Paris, the Place de la Concorde, there is the
figure of a majestically beautiful woman, seated. She
symbolizes the province of Alsace, on the border between France and Germany. For centuries Alsace has
been the shuttlecock of war between the two countries.

passing from one to the other, then back again. In 1870 it was still French soil, but France was fighting Germany once more, and on a day in June of the following year a sad procession of men, women, and children filled the Place de la Concorde. While workmen draped the statue of Alsace in black, many in the great crowd wept. France had lost her province again. The statue of Alsace seemed unmoved, but the black drapery stirring in the wind gave the figure an eerily human look.

Albert Schweitzer's parents were still childless at the time. As Alsatians, they became German subjects overnight. But when Albert was born four years later they saw to it that French was as much his language as German. He was not exceptional in this; most children in Alsace were equally at home in both languages.

Even when he was six years old the historic change that had taken place in Alsace mattered little to him. What was important was that his sky and earth had remained unchanged.

To Alsatians their land is the most beautiful on earth. Even allowing for regional pride, the fact is that Alsace is the kind of countryside that makes men speak feelingly of their own countries in such terms as "sweet land," "homeland," "fatherland," and "motherland."

For Albert Schweitzer, at the age of six, Alsace was only Günsbach, a small village—it seemed big to him—and the hills that sheltered it.

But let us follow him on a typical summer picnic when Pastor Schweitzer took Albert and several other children, too young to be at school, for a day in the hills. With knapsacks full of good things to eat, the party left the parsonage and passed through a village of picture-book houses with outside stairways and other features mellowed with the centuries.

On the road the party had to step aside for a parade of fat geese led by a pompous gander. For those who are fond of fancy foods, these Alsatian geese are world-famous for that great delicacy, *pâte de foie gras*, they furnish. Famous, too, are the sleek cattle the party passed in the fields, for this is the valley of Münster, and it produces the cheese that is named after it and is being imitated, in vain, the world over.

And just as famous are the vineyards that mantle the hills with a glow of gold at ripening time. They make the white Alsatian wines that are loved far beyond its borders. On such a hot day as that of the picnic the sun distills a fragrance from the vineyards. It mingles with the tang in the air from the tobacco fields all around, and with all the other sweet smells ranging from the honey scent of buckwheat in bloom to perfumes from orchards and flower gardens blazing in the sun.

There is so much nectar in Alsace that Albert saw bees winging heavily home to their hives looking as if they were overloaded with it.

He also watched cream-colored oxen and handsome horses pull towering hay wagons, the carters either dozing on top or walking alongside, with whips draped about their shoulders like some ornament of office. Had

13

the boy seen one of the animals lashed, the sight would have cut through him as though it were his own flesh that had been treated so, but in Alsace these whips are little more than traditional costume.

The other children on the picnic were too impatient to be spectators only, and Albert soon joined them in activity. They flopped belly down on banks of crystal-clear brooks with pebbly bottoms, to launch the ships they had brought along, each the shell of half a walnut.

They waded into ponds after water lilies, some silver-white, others pink, but all heady with scent. They raced headlong down the hills, practically on wings, knowing that even if they did tumble it would be into soft beds of sweet grass or wild strawberry. They rolled like barrels down the steepest slopes. And, hot and grimy, they splashed into a little lake that had been blue with sky.

Of these picnics Albert Schweitzer wrote later, "And thus we grew up like a bunch of wild roses."

In the distance there sounded a muffled grumbling: Pastor Schweitzer looked up at the silver-edged thunderheads and shepherded his flock toward home.

They passed the village schoolhouse just in time to see its pupils break out of it like excited sparrows. To Albert, coming from a day on the hills, it seemed that they had been pent up in prison. They raced for their homes, their wooden shoes clattering, and almost immediately reappeared in windows munching chunks of bread.

Albert got home just as the downpour came. It made

music for him, the drumming on the roof, the whispering against the panes, a swelling crescendo when the
wind came howling; then as the shower abated there
was a chuckling in the rain pipes and a sound like tiny
bells as drops fell one by one into a barrel.

Some tune catches you and for a time refuses to
leave. With Albert it was often that way, snatches of
some song he had heard or a tune from some composition of his own. Or he would be trying to weave music
out of whatever came to his ears at the time and appealed to him.

Just then he was listening to the sounds that came
from outside the parsonage, now that the rain had
stopped. The town crier was beating his drum to call
attention to his announcements. A peddler was blow-
ing a horn. There was a jingling of goat bells and a
babel of bleating as a flock came down from the hills
with milk for sale, and the goatherd had a horn, too.
Birds that had been cheeping under the eaves when
they were rainbound now found full voice again. And
from the church tower came evening bells.

Any youngster home from a rich day wants to tell
about it, and Albert felt like the bees he had seen that
day, full of what he had been gathering. But what can
you do when you are so young that you still lack many
words? Years later you will learn that there never have
been words for many of the things you feel.

Albert wanted to tell his mother all that he had seen
and smelled and relished and done and thought and
felt that day. He tried it, taking deep breaths, but all

15

that came were a few words that got in one another's way. His mother said she understood perfectly, but Albert did not see how she could, with the little that he had been able to tell about it, so he wandered off by himself to the big, square piano.

For some months Pastor Schweitzer had been giving Albert lessons on it, and at first it was as if his father were trying to introduce him to an old friend about whom he had learned much by himself. Then the lessons became exciting with newness, and Pastor Schweitzer was himself excited by the boy's greed and speed of learning.

Since words had been so poor in telling what the day had been, Albert now felt about the keys to see what the piano could do, except that he pretended it was the organ in his father's church. He found two notes together which, if trilled fast enough, sounded a little like a heavily laden bee. The treble came near saying, "We're birds!" The bass notes grumbled somewhat like that soft summer thunder in the hills. The church bells were easy to imitate, but not the feeling they gave him. That eluded him no matter how much he tried.

But on the whole it was all much easier than words. That was one day.

There were many other days, quite like it, except that he never could take their riches for granted. But, not knowing any better, he thought that their heavenly freedom would last forever.

Genius in the Jungle

Until the morning Pastor Schweitzer put a slate under the boy's arm and led him, weeping bitterly, off
to that prison of a school.

LIGHT snow was falling, the first of the winter, the
air lit a glow in the blood, school had just let out,
and the small boy looked hungrily on while all his
schoolmates went quite crazy. They whooped with
laughter over nothing at all, chased each other for no
good reason, ran races they did not finish, or fell to
wrestling apparently without caring who won.

The small boy's pride and reserve were having a
hard time of it, and his eyes showed it. Every muscle
and nerve in him craved to join the hurly-burly. But
how can you jump into play where you are not
wanted?

He had not been in that school long enough for the

others to know what he was really like, but they were sure they knew. He was dressed somewhat better than the village boys, so he must be rich. He was shy, but they were certain he *chose* to stay aloof. He was the pastor's son, so he must think himself superior. Very well, let him enjoy his superiority all by himself.

He had tried being by himself, but that snowfall and the commotion the boys made over it proved too much for him. He walked up to the biggest boy there, George Nitschelm, red-faced, brawny, and considerably heavier than Albert.

"I'll wrestle you," Albert said, "and I bet I win."

He said it in a way that should have won him friends at once. His smile was something to see, then and throughout his life, a friendliness that came from the depths, shone in the eyes, and suffused his face.

George Nitschelm stared at him, then hooted with anticipation. He spat on his hands, grinned at the circle of faces that had closed about them, and shouted, "Come on, my fine gentleman!"

It was a term of contempt. It meant that you were not of the people, but "gentry," enjoying luxuries you did not deserve, but, since everything was so soft for you, it followed that you must be soft yourself, body and character.

The smile on Albert's face fled, and in its place there was a look of desperation. He must prove them wrong, he must show them that he was in no way different from them and deserved to be admitted to their world as an equal in everything.

Genius in the Jungle

He flung himself at George.

From the first it was clear that the parson's son knew little about rough-and-tumble wrestling. The onlookers howled with glee as they saw "gentry" getting the worst of it. Repeatedly George slammed him down, fell on him, and tried to pin his shoulders to the ground.

But muscle alone will carry one only so far when all that is at stake is play or show-off. Besides, George did not feel he needed to exert himself against the parson's son. At first it looked as though he were right.

But if in a struggle you are so desperate about something that it becomes a life-and-death matter, then you can draw on strength reserved by nature for emergencies. It became a life-and-death matter for Albert to win that wrestling match. But most things seemed to matter greatly to him, so that he poured every last ounce of strength into whatever task was before him.

Fortunately for him, though he was not so heavy as George, he was nevertheless big-boned and powerful for his age. What was more, he had a mind like lightning. George's wrestling tricks worked almost up to the last moment needed for victory. But by then there flashed into the other boy's mind and muscles the feel of what to do, and he would slip out of George's clutches.

The glee of the crowd grew uncertain. It was taking their champion longer to win than they had expected. George himself was no longer contemptuous, and several times he had the wind knocked out of him.

The parson's son was catching up. And quite suddenly but decisively he slammed George down on his back and kept his shoulders down, so that an honest count would have declared him the winner.

His face streaked with sweat and mud, Albert looked down with a smile at the prostrate boy. There was no sign of gloating in the smile, only a friendly look waiting for the other to acknowledge a plain fact.

Instead there was a whine. "Well, if we had as much to eat at home as you, I'd have licked you!"

Albert could not believe what he had heard, and he looked up at the others. Surely *they* wouldn't believe so obvious an excuse.

He saw that they did believe it.

Without a word he got to his feet and ran home.

His family was startled at his appearance and waited to hear what had happened. They did not hear it from him. He washed and changed but did not come down until supper. Even then he said nothing, but the family respected his silence.

His mother had meanwhile added one of his favorite dishes. Albert did not touch it. Innocent that he was, he was visualizing George Nitschelm at home like himself at dinner but with almost nothing to eat. In his imagination he saw the other boys, too, their supper tables as bare as George's, and for the first time he saw the barrier between them and him.

Desperately he wanted that barrier down, to be one of them. But what could he do about it? He could not feed a whole village. Then another thought struck him. The snowfall that had seemed so zestful he now saw

Genius in the Jungle

as a reminder that winter was near. The village tailor was at work on a warm overcoat for him. How many of his schoolmates would have overcoats at all when the bitter weather came? They had howled with glee when they saw his face pushed into the mud. Now he could look forward to seeing their faces blue with cold. Revenge is sweet when you have been badly hurt, but something robbed the boy of pleasure in such revenge. Instead he cringed at the thought of how cold they would be. . . .

There was to be a special service at the church the following Sunday, and the tailor was hurrying to get the boy's overcoat ready for the occasion. He sent for Albert to come for a fitting.

The boy did not look enthusiastic when the overcoat was tried on him.

"What's the matter?" the tailor asked. "Don't you like it? Why, see what a fine-looking gentleman you are!"

Albert did not answer.

At the parsonage next Sunday the family waited to see how he would look in his new overcoat. He refused to put it on. His father asked why.

"I'd rather not wear it," Albert said.

His father's face clouded. "By any chance is it because it's made over from my old coat?"

A country parson with a big family to feed cannot always afford a new overcoat for a boy.

"It's not that," Albert said.

"What then?"

"The other boys have no overcoats."

"But you have one."

"I'm sorry."

"That's an admirable sentiment, but put the coat on," his father said. "I won't have the congregation think that my son has no winter overcoat."

Albert did not move.

His father came closer. "You *refuse* to wear it?"

"I won't wear an overcoat."

"Then you know what I'm compelled to do?"

"Yes."

His father boxed his ears.

But the same action may mean different things. A box on the ears may mean a wish to hurt. Or it may be only a set manner of dealing with a given situation. In Günsbach you did such things according to the manners and customs of the people. If a son disobeyed you, you boxed his ears. But there was a limit to the punishment any boy deserved in such circumstances.

Albert went to church that Sunday without an overcoat, and every Sunday thereafter even in bad weather. Each time he received the same punishment, no more, no less.

Albert's mother knew what the congregation was thinking: that their parson's son was not dressed according to his station. She winced at it, but she said nothing to Albert about it.

About this time she took him for a visit to Strasbourg, the capital of Alsace. Albert's hat was not suitable for the occasion, so she took him to the best store in the city to buy him another. She selected a sailor hat. He refused to put it on. The clerk tried one kind after another, with no better luck. Finally exasperated, he demanded of Albert, "What kind of hat *do* you want?"

Albert told him. The clerk protested. "Why, you'd look like an ordinary village boy!"

But Albert insisted it was that or no other.

"Well, we don't sell that kind of hat," the clerk said loftily.

Albert looked relieved. But his mother asked the clerk whether he could not send out and get the kind of hat the boy wanted.

"But, my dear madam!" the clerk protested.

In the end Albert wore the kind of cap the village boys in Günsbach wore, and was greatly pleased. His mother was not, but she understood.

5

EVERY time the village postman entered the parsonage yard the Schweitzers' sizable dog tried to get at him. The animal was not chained, and it was Albert's task to protect the man. With a stick dramatically poised he would back the dog into a corner of the yard and stand over him looking much like a lion tamer at work, and feeling quite as important.

But the dog had a spirit of his own and occasionally tried to rush past Albert, and each time the stick taught him better. He slunk back cowering. It would have reassured him, however, had he known how sick at heart Albert felt.

The boy had done what a disciplined mind had told him must be done, but always there was that feeling.

About this time a neighbor took him for a ride in a farm cart behind an old horse. Excited by his high place at the driver's side, the boy asked for more speed. The farmer obliged by whipping the horse. The old animal's flanks heaved, and his limp showed what a cruel demand he was meeting, and the sight cost the boy all the pleasure he had been feeling.

On another occasion the farmer let the boy take the horse out alone. This time Albert allowed the animal to go slowly. They had just passed a lane when a big dog in a fury sprang at the horse, which reared up in panic.

Albert had a long whip in his hand, and before he could stop himself he had struck at the dog. He had meant only to frighten him off, but his aim was better than he had expected, and the lash caught the dog in the eye. Howling with pain, the animal rolled over and over in the road.

For weeks the boy could hardly sleep.

It was at this time that he composed an addition to the bedtime prayer that had been taught him. It had seemed unfair to him that animals should be left out of it, and at the end of it he used to whisper, "And, please, Heavenly Father, protect and bless *all* living creatures."

A cruel test of the sincerity of his own feeling toward them came just when life seemed to be taking on a happy aspect. His schoolmates were accepting him as an equal, although he was still on trial. At any rate, one fine spring morning they invited him to come along on a hunting party. They were all equipped with home-made slingshots, and they gave him one. At target practice he proved he was good.

His spirits soared as he tramped off into the hills with his friends, looking for birds to bring down. They came on a treetop full of them singing their heads off.

Albert Schweitzer

The hunting party excitedly surrounded the birds and took aim. One of them whispered, "Hey, Albert, you're nearest. Let's see you get that big one."

Albert was nearest the birds and could see them, vivid against a turquoise sky. They had speckled brown breasts, their wings were edged with crimson, and their throats throbbed with song. He would shoot wide of the mark, of course, and no one would suspect anything. But any moment now the others would let loose a volley and some of these birds would come tumbling.

Albert was in agony.

At that moment there came the windy clangor of church bells caroling so jubilantly that even the starlings that lived in the steeple must have been startled. To Albert it was the providentially timed answer to a prayer, and he gave a cry that *could* be mistaken by the others as mere excitement of the hunt. But it scattered the birds on the treetop before a single slingshot could come anywhere near them.

Schweitzer wrote afterward: "The music drove the Commandment into my heart, 'Thou shalt not kill!' It was one of the great experiences of my childhood and youth."

But his companions of the hunt felt differently about it. They looked at Albert with anger and suspicion. He held his breath. Would he lose his newly won friends?

For the time being he did not.

But not long after that, an old Jew came to Günsbach on business in his donkey cart. His visits were always a hilarious occasion for the village boys. They surrounded his cart, shouting and jeering. Each boy pulled a bit of shirt or jacket through his fist until the cloth looked like a pig's ear, a bit of Jew-baiting familiar to children in that part of the world.

In his anxiety to keep his friends Albert did as they did. They pursued the cart out of the village as far as the bridge. When Albert got close to the cart he saw a gray-bearded old man with a freckled face turn and smile at them, patiently, good-naturedly, but with embarrassment.

"The smile overpowered me," Schweitzer wrote later.

The result was that one day when the old Jew came to Günsbach the whole village saw Albert greet him with a handshake and walk by the donkey cart chatting with him like an old friend.

The Jew was puzzled by the boy's friendliness, and never did learn the reason unless many years later he chanced to read Albert Schweitzer's memoirs.

6

HAPPILY Albert's act of independence did not cost him as dearly as he thought it would. His schoolmates still accepted him, partly because the parson's son did not make so good a showing in school as most of them did. He had real difficulty in reading and writing, and many years later his comment on the village boys was that they "had at least as much in their heads as I had in mine. . . . One was better at mental arithmetic; another made fewer mistakes in his dictation; a third never forgot a date; still another always topped me in geography. . . ."

But how can you pay attention to mental arithmetic or to historical dates when your mind is still roaming in freedom on the hills, or you are quailing at the memory of a dog rolling in pain in the road because your whip had caught him in the eye; or when on happier days you are reveling in imagination, seated in "Daddy" Iltis's place at the organ?

So you take what comfort you can out of the fact that your teacher's impatience with your slowness in learning makes you all the more acceptable by your schoolmates who feel superior.

But one day Albert almost lost his prestige as a "regular" boy. He was standing in front of the class when from an adjoining room there came the sound of children singing in harmony. He had never heard two-part singing before and suddenly he felt faint, his knees began to give way, and he had to prop himself against the wall to keep from falling.

One may well ask what was the matter with him. Were the voices so exquisite and the music so overwhelming? They were the voices of children he knew, and the song was familiar. Was he, then, still sickly? It could hardly be that, since the puny infant who had won out against death was now a rugged boy with a deep chest and a spread of shoulders. Then he must be emotionally easy to upset? Hardly, for he was already foreshadowing in character the man who eventually was to stand up against everything that two world wars and a savage continent were to throw at him.

Press against a door with all your weight and if it flies open you fall. Or suppose you have been bracing yourself night and day for years against the pressure, say, of war, or the conviction that life is devastating. "As far back as I can remember," Albert Schweitzer wrote, "I had been saddened by the amount of misery in the world around me." Again he was not exceptional in this.

Then suppose that suddenly out of the blue for a fleeting moment there comes complete illusion that all cruelty has vanished from the world and that you are hearing humanity singing in heavenly harmony. It would not be surprising if for the duration of that moment you were almost literally caught off balance—which was what had happened to the boy.

When Albert had recovered his composure, he felt so dismayed at himself that he determined never again to betray his emotions that way.

But he was equally determined to recapture that exquisite moment if he could.

He threw himself into music studies with such passion that his father soon found it necessary to get him a more professional teacher and, since it was the organ rather than the piano that Albert dreamed about, Pastor Schweitzer had "Daddy" Iltis take his place.

The first time the boy sat down at the organ at the side of "Daddy" Iltis his feet could barely reach the pedals.

His teacher showed him what the different keys would do when touched, then told him to play a few notes.

The boy froze with fear. He was afraid of the thunder, the silver trumpets, and the golden voices that would roar in protest at the touch of a blundering fool.

"Go on, my boy," his teacher smiled. "You play the piano, this isn't so very different. Try it."

Albert tried it, and, for all his resolution never to let any circumstance unnerve him, it happened again.

He spent countless hours thereafter at the console

of that instrument, until he thought he was at home with it.

Nevertheless on a Sunday morning two years later he was just as much afraid as the first time he had sat down at the organ. There was a special reason for it that Sunday. For the first time he was alone up there, while the church was full below. Some of his father's congregation who had been slack in attending church were there that day to hear the parson's son play at the services for the first time.

In the mirror Albert saw his father come down from the pulpit, and there was a hush while the congregation waited for the organ.

The pause seemed longer than usual, then there was uneasiness. Something was holding the organist back.

Suddenly the sonorous prelude of an old hymn swelled on the air, purely played, surprising in its maturity, and the congregation joined in, singing perhaps with more of a lift in their voices than usual.

7

THE small schoolhouse in Günsbach was not enough of a school for its pupils after the first two years, so when Albert was nine he and some of his schoolmates had to go to a bigger one in the town of Münster two miles away. They went there and back on foot, together at first, but after the first few weeks Albert avoided company on these walks.

He had outgrown his need for the companionship of his schoolmates in his now greater need to be alone as he worked out answers to the many questions that were seething in his mind.

Some of them developed out of the Bible stories that Pastor Schaffler, one of the teachers at the Münster school, would render so dramatically that he himself was moved to tears by some and laughed with exhilaration at others.

Though Albert felt with him, he did not weep with him, restraining himself from what he felt would be an unseemly show of feeling on his part, but he did laugh aloud at the other stories. It was the laughter of

Genius in the Jungle

a boy overflowing with vitality, and was so explosive that Pastor Schaffler nicknamed him Isaac, Hebrew for "the laugher," whereupon Albert tried to restrain himself in that, too, especially as his schoolmates poked fun at him for it.

But whatever emotions the stories had aroused in him, they did not affect the robust realism of the questions they raised in his mind. He was deeply moved, for instance, by the pastor's reading of the birth of the infant Jesus in the manger, and the visits there of the shepherds and the Wise Men who came bearing gifts of "gold and frankincense, and myrrh."

Albert asked why the infant's mother and her husband still remained poor after such a visit. And didn't the Wise Men look in on the family afterward? And what about the shepherds who had come in such worshipful wonder, why didn't they remain excited enough to go everywhere and tell the story of the great Coming?

He asked many such questions. But the answers did not satisfy him, so he wanted privacy on his walks to and from school to think things over.

In addition, Albert had already absorbed enough history of Alsace to feel strongly about the many wars that had raged over his countryside. (He did not dream, of course, that in his own lifetime two more wars, the most devastating in all history, were to sweep back and forth across Alsace.)

How could anyone have the heart to destroy such humble homes, to murder so much? And since so many people had been worshiping the Prince of Peace over so many centuries, why were there still so many wars?

Such questions are heavy fare for a boy walking through a smiling countryside, and he would literally shake his head to throw them off.

It was not hard to do it at first. He looked up to the Münster hills and saw topping them the remains of an ancient castle and of an abbey—structures that had teemed with life a thousand years and some centuries before. There was a roaring stream that boiled up into cataracts and wound about in the valley, and it somehow blended with the ruins on the skyline.

In the spring the waking countryside excited Albert with its new green and the voices of birds just back from the south. A little later there was the glow of blossoms in the orchards, and the gardens were already masses of color.

Summer, with its vacation time, gave him still more variety on his walks alone. A royal stag and he stared at each other in surprise for a moment at the edge of a pine forest. Other wild life darted unexpectedly from thickets and deep grass.

But what moved him most was the human cycle of the year, the ploughing and the sowing in the spring, the ripening of the blond fields of wheat in the late summer, and the harvesting in the fall. Best of all was when the vineyards were ready. Then girls and women in colorful skirts and bodices worked along with the men, carrying great baskets of white grapes to the wagons waiting for them in the shades of giant oaks, and they all sang as they worked.

He even helped some men who were building a house, adding his muscles to theirs in heaving heavy beams into place.

It all gave him such a glow that he wished he could communicate it to others.

Albert would have been helped by the poet Browning, when he wrote of David, the minstrel shepherd of the Bible, singing to King Saul to bring him out of his deep depression.

". . . Then I played the help-tune of our reapers,
  their wine-song, when hand
Grasps at hand, eye lights eye in good friendship,
  and great hearts expand
And grow one in the sense of this world's life. . . .

     . . . .

. . . And then the great march
Wherein man runs to man to assist him and buttress
                an arch
Naught can break; . . .

     . . . .

How good is man's life, the mere living! how fit to
  employ
All the heart and the soul and the senses, for ever
  in joy!"

He even tried his own hand at saying it with poetry.
"But I never got further than the first two or three

rhymes. Once or twice, too, I tried my hand at sketching the hills, with the old castle which rose on the other side of the valley, but that too was a failure."

But when he got home he would hurry to the organ loft in his father's church.

There he had wings, there he knew what angels must feel as they travel daily through heavenly landscapes and, never ceasing to wonder at them, simply have to sing hosannas to let everyone know how it all feels.

8

WHEN Albert was through with elementary school his mother packed his things, and the boy took a train for Mülhausen, to enter high school, the *Gymnasium* there. Again he wept, secretly, of course, at leaving behind the life he loved, and this time he had somewhat better reason to mourn the past.

He would be spending the next four years in the

home of his godfather, Louis Schweitzer, and his wife. Herr Schweitzer was director of the elementary schools in the city, and his wife had been a schoolteacher. They should have known children well, but they were childless, and to them children were only young creatures to be trained by hard work and discipline. They had strong convictions about the bad effects of idle moments, and they saw to it that their young kinsman was kept busy.

All morning and every morning but Sundays there was school; lunch was brief so that there would be some time for piano practice; then school again in the afternoon; and in the evening, homework and more piano practice. Sunday was free only for a short and formal walk about the city with Aunt Sophie.

It is not surprising, therefore, that Albert got little more than daydreams out of his classes. It became his godfather's painful duty to send for Pastor Schweitzer and report that his son was doing so poorly in school that it would be only right to give his place to some boy more fit for higher education.

Pastor Schweitzer did not scold his son, knowing that there was no lack of seriousness in him. He was puzzled, but prevailed on the godfather to give the boy another chance, which he did.

It was a new teacher who worked the change in Albert. The man put so much enthusiasm into his work that soon Albert's marks showed the boy's response.

And one Sunday when spring was particularly lovely, Aunt Sophie looked at the boy hard at work on his lessons, and said, "It's too fine a day to spend indoors. Come along and I'll show you as beautiful country as you have at Günsbach."

Thereafter Albert's home in Mülhausen no longer seemed a prison.

9

BUT he was in trouble—with music, of all things. Eugene Münsch, a young teacher fresh from a conservatory, was giving Albert piano lessons and found him "a thorn in the flesh," as he put it, a pupil who seemed to have neither mind nor heart for music. He judged this from the fact that Aunt Sophie kept the boy hard at practice and yet, when it came to playing an as-

signed lesson, Albert either did not know it even pass-
ably, or he played it woodenly.

Finally one day Herr Münsch assigned one of the
simplest possible compositions for the boy's next lesson. "I suppose you will butcher it as you do everything else you play," he said irascibly. "But I can't help
it. If a boy has no feeling I can't give him any."

He did not know that the trouble with Albert was
too much feeling. The compositions that had been given
him to study were so lifeless for him that instead of
practicing them the boy would wander off on music
that meant more to him.

Then, too, music was his most private dwelling place,
and he found it hard to open his heart to strangers.
Besides, he did not quite know what was going on in
himself, and he didn't want others to know of his confusion. He was entering the borderland between boyhood and manhood, a time when even the voice changes
so unexpectedly that it becomes embarrassing. Just as
you have begun to feel good about the new deeper note
in it, your voice suddenly betrays you by going up in
the air.

But when Herr Münsch accused Albert of a lack of
feeling for music it was something that no boy on the
way to manhood could take. Without saying a word
to Herr Münsch he pounced on the new piece assigned
to him, and what he did not learn about playing it in
the course of the next two weeks was not worth
knowing.

When the time came for him to play the composition, he saw that his teacher was braced for the worst. But after the first few bars Herr Münsch looked surprised.

When the last note had died away it took the teacher some time to gather his thoughts. He put his hand on the boy's shoulder and took his place at the piano. Herr Münsch then played a much more advanced composition, not so much as a lesson but as a tribute to Albert's playing.

Not long after that he took Albert to St. Stephen's Church, where Herr Münsch was the organist, and gave him lessons on the instrument which drew large audiences there. Albert himself went to his teacher's recitals, and was proud to be his pupil.

He was still prouder when Herr Münsch let him play the organ at St. Stephen's Church, although there was no one but the teacher to hear him.

He must have played well indeed, and made much progress, for a great Sunday came when the youth, still in his teens, performed on the famous organ before an audience that filled the big church to the outermost door.

"Thus came fulfillment of a dream," Schweitzer wrote, "long cherished in secret."

One day when teacher and pupil were alone in the organ loft Herr Münsch said, "Now I'll play you a composition you have probably never heard before."

He played something that was new indeed to the boy. Albert had learned to recognize a great composer

by his style even though a given selection was unknown
to him. But this composer he did not know.

All he knew was that never had music moved him so
profoundly.

"Who is it?" he asked. "Who wrote it?"

Herr Münsch told him that the composer had been
dead nearly a century and a half, but that even in his
own lifetime his music had been dismissed as old-fashioned, and when he died his music seemed to have died
with him. Many years later, however, it was discovered
by some of the world's greatest musicians. It was ironic
that the man who had seemed old-fashioned in his own
time should inspire so many greatly gifted young men
generations later. Mozart, who had been composing
since early childhood, was excited by him. Beethoven,
at the age of ten, played the forgotten composer at his
concerts. Mendelssohn was only twelve when he discovered a manuscript of the dead man's and did not
rest until years later he got together three hundred and
fifty voices to sing one of the man's "old-fashioned"
choral works. Chopin played him. And all these young
geniuses, consciously and unconsciously, wove what
they had learned from the dead man into their own
deathless compositions.

One would think that all this was enough to wake
a world. Yet even as Herr Münsch was telling it all
to Albert there were only a handful of music lovers
to let the world know what it was missing.

Herr Münsch proposed now that Albert should join

the devoted few in helping the dead composer win the world-wide audience and the immortality he so deserved.

Albert needed no more urging than a young bird that has just discovered wings needs to be urged to fly.

10

THE German word for a brook is surely a poor name for the huge family that has for centuries poured out so great a flood of music as the Bachs. Albert Schweitzer, digging into its history—there was little written until that time—learned that as far back as the 1500's there was a German miller and baker, Veit Bach, whose zither "sounded very pretty amidst the clattering of the millwheels." His son was the first in the family to turn professional musician. Then, for one generation of Bachs after another, there followed such a procession of violinists, cellists, choir leaders, concertmasters, church organists, and composers that in one city the word for any musician was a *Bach*.

But the man in whose service young Albert Schweitzer had enlisted was the greatest of them all, Johann Sebastian Bach. Today it is hard to realize how little he was known as late as sixty years ago, when Albert had set out to know him through and through.

In several respects he had a good start. He, too, knew what it was to have had musicians in the family for generations. His father played the organ as well as the piano. Grandfathers on both sides were organists, as were several of their brothers.

Bach had played the church organ. The young Albert knew what it was to play it; and at the height of Schweitzer's career, competent critics declared him to be one of the great organists of our time—in recital and as a recording artist as well.

Bach composed some of his most affecting music, the Chorales, to the words of simple folk hymns. Albert had been moved by such hymns from his first days.

Then there was the basic fact that Bach was a deeply religious man. There is the famous story of the humble juggler, who wanted desperately to pay some tribute to God, but he was poor at words and poorer still in pocket, so he went to the famous shrine of Notre Dame and offered up the best he had, his juggling act. Bach offered up an incomparably greater gift, but deep at heart the two had felt alike. "For Bach," Schweitzer wrote, "music is an act of worship."

This, too, Schweitzer understood deeply.

Albert Schweitzer

He gave himself over to the study of Bach, the man and the composer, and to the playing of the organ, so that by the time he was eighteen Herr Münsch had told him he must now go to one of the greatest teachers there was, Charles Marie Widor, organist at the Church of St. Sulpice in Paris.

A month later Albert was in Paris. The country boy was so bewildered that on the day he was to meet Widor for the first time he came late. Apologetically the youth's first words were, "May I play you something?"

"Play what?"

"Bach, of course."

The teacher's face lit up. He was one of the small brotherhood of Bach worshipers. He heard Albert play, and took him on as a pupil, free.

Not only was the teacher rewarded by it, but the world was as well. For the day came when the teacher turned to the pupil for guidance on Bach.

It seems that in the Chorales Widor understood the composer so long as the music was only the introduction, the prelude to a hymn. But the music of the hymn itself baffled the teacher. Why did Bach do so and so in the structure of the hymn itself?

Schweitzer asked if Widor knew the words that went with the music. Widor said no. Schweitzer, who knew the hymns by heart, translated them for him.

At once Bach became illuminated.

"The relation of Bach's music to its text," Schweitzer wrote later, "is the most intimate that can be imag-

imed. . . . If the text speaks of drifting mists, of bois-
terous winds, of roaring rivers, of waves that ebb and
flow, of leaves falling from the trees, of bells that ring
for the dying, of the confident faith that walks with
firm steps, or the weak faith that falters insecure, of the
proud who will be abased and the humble who will be
exalted, of Satan rising in rebellion, of angels poised on
the clouds of heaven, then one hears and sees all this in
his music. . . . Joy, sorrow, tears, lamentation, laughter, to all these it gives voice. . . ."

Widor asked Schweitzer to write a little essay that
would thus clarify the playing of much of Bach's music.
The "little essay" became the two-volume work that is
considered the most brilliant introduction to Bach that
has yet appeared.

Then at concerts in the musical capitals of Europe
and in his recordings Schweitzer conveyed on the organ
what his book conveyed with words.

Life as it unfolded itself to him now seemed indeed
"fit to employ all the heart and the soul and the senses
forever in joy."

The trouble was that Schweitzer would always be
the man who in his boyhood could not eat his supper
because he imagined that others in the village had less
than he or nothing to eat.

"Ever more clearly there presented itself the question to me whether happiness was a thing that I might
accept as a matter of course. And an experience joined
itself to it . . . one that has accompanied me from my
childhood up, my deep sympathy with the pain that

prevails in the world around us. These two experiences slowly merged, and thence came a decision as to the future of my life. . . ."

11

ALBERT came back to Mülhausen to face the full faculty of the Gymnasium in an oral examination that was to decide how high he would graduate that year. It was always a formal and formidable affair, and one had to dress accordingly. Albert had inherited a frock coat that would be suitable, but not the trousers, so he borrowed a pair from an uncle. The man was short, and Albert was tall. He lengthened his suspenders with string, but even then the trousers barely reached his shoetops.

When Albert came into the crowded examination hall and marched up to face the faculty there was a roar of laughter from the students, and even some of the faculty had to hide their smiles. But Professor Albrecht, who was in charge of the examination, did not find the occasion funny and said so. For him the "merriment was irreverent," and since Albert was the cause of it he made it hard for him in the examination.

He asked, for instance, a detailed account of how a certain fleet in ancient times had been maneuvered in a certain battle. Albert had not been interested in the subject and did not know. Professor Albrecht denounced such ignorance as a "serious defect in culture." Albert's mental comment, as he later reported, was that it was "a more serious defect in culture that we were leaving the Gymnasium without knowing anything about astronomy and geology."

The last subject of the examination was Professor Albrecht's own specialty, and he asked Albert to compare the colonization methods of the ancient Greeks to those of the Romans. That question had body to it and made sense to Albert.

The result was that the answers left Professor Albrecht beaming, and Albert Schweitzer ended his Gymnasium years on a note of triumph.

12

ALBERT went straight to the famous University of Strasbourg. He climbed the tower of the world-renowned Cathedral and looked down on the city, mellowed and picturesque with seventeen hundred years of history: peaked roofs with their stork nests, wooden verandas gay with flower boxes and murmurous with dovecots. Beyond them were the canals, villages, and fertile fields of the Rhine valley, and the broad, shining ribbon of the fabled river itself. Beyond that in turn was the Black Forest, home of legends and regal stags, with the huntsman's horn still sounding in the heart of the great woods.

He found a room in a house in the Old Fish Market. He did not know at the time that over a century before another youth had come to Strasbourg to study and had lived in that very room; that he, too, had climbed the Cathedral tower and, looking forward, had found life overflowing with promise.

Life more than made good its promises to young Johann Wolfgang Goethe. In the long years it gave him

Genius in the Jungle

he became the greatest poet since Shakespeare, and made careers for himself as lawyer, scientist, painter, critic, novelist, soldier, theatrical director, political economist, philosopher, mathematician, administrator, and statesman.

Schweitzer would never be the universal genius that Goethe had been, but he was a greater artist in music than Goethe was at painting, and he far surpassed him in strength of character and in his compassion for suffering humanity. Nevertheless Schweitzer came to understand Goethe so well that shortly thereafter he won a prize and, later, world-wide acclaim, for his interpretation of the man, his life, and his spirit.

When he came to the university, Schweitzer was already deep in Greek and Latin, and now he added Hebrew to his studies. He found the language difficult at first, which was all he needed to make him master it. He also enrolled in the faculties of philosophy and theology, and in all took on a program that would have broken the back of an ordinary student. But then, his day had more hours in it than that of other students. When the others slept, Schweitzer delighted in staying up night after night studying, until his fellow students and the faculty decided that he could not be human.

In addition to his studies, there were the many hours of rehearsals on the organ and the recitals he gave in one country after another.

At this time he was called for the year of military service that Germany required of its educated young men. He went off with a Greek Bible in his knapsack.

Albert Schweitzer

All that year during drills, strenuous marches, and other physically exhausting activities, his body would be doing one thing, his mind another. After twelve to sixteen hours of training, his fellow conscripts were glad to call it a day. But Schweitzer would stay up to ask searching questions of his Bible, and since his researches had not furnished satisfactory answers, he tried to work out his own.

When the year of military service was up, he returned to the university, and soon theological circles were discussing the young man who dared dispute august authorities but whose challenge had to be met.

The historic bells of the Cathedral which sounded the hours were mostly unheard by him. By day he was too absorbed in studies. Evenings he spent in talk with fellow students and professors, talk that was music to his mind, rich with harmonies, and stimulating even in its discords. After the others had gone to bed Schweitzer would go to his room to study and to write. The morning sun found him still at it, seemingly as fresh as though he had slept all night.

He made up for lost sleep, however, on week ends and on vacations at the parsonage in Günsbach, which was only a short train ride from the university. Even then for several nights there would be late hours of talk with his family.

One Whitsunday morning at home he awoke slowly out of a deep sleep, every last sinew in him so rested that he could have sung. Sunlight streaming through shaggy foliage played on the walls of his room. He

Genius in the Jungle

could see apple blossoms and lilacs, and their scents came wafting in. Birdsong overflowed, and the breeze brought the sound of organ practice in the church, then the steeple bells rang in the festival day that it was.

He lay listening to it all and to his happiness. How generously life had dealt with him, how lavishly! A powerful body, abounding health, a teeming mind, music in every fiber, a score of skills, and a driving energy that knew no rest—nor did it seem to need any. His dearest daydreams had more than come true, and from every side there came assurance that it was all only a foretaste of what the future would be. . . .

It was too great fortune to take for granted.

His thoughts turned to the many, far too many, who had little or nothing. . . . Such sunless, poverty-stricken lives . . . bodies that had never known well-being and were little more than carriers of sickness and pain . . . minds that lived in darkness and in fear. . . . Their only dreams that did come true were nightmares. . . .

How can one have the heart to be given much and not go and share *some* of it with those others . . . much of it . . . all of it?

"To whom much is given, of him shall much be required. . . . Freely you have received, freely give. . . . Preach the word . . . heal the sick. . . ."

An honest man does not disregard such commandments. . . . He goes to those who have little and stays with them until he has made a difference in their lives. . . . How long? As long as there is misery to be relieved. . . . But there is so much of it in the world that it may swallow up a lifetime to cope with even a small part of it! . . . Well, others have done it. He had been given more than his share. Was he to hoard it all?

But other voices in him protested that talents, too, were entitled to life, growth, and fulfillment. His were only half realized. . . . He owed them something, too. . . .

He came to his decision. He would devote the next nine years to music and to science, to teaching and to preaching, and to other "necessities of my being." Then he would put it all behind him and seek out some benighted area where he could be of direct service, "man to man," to those who had so much less than he. . . .

He was twenty-one at the time. This meant—if he kept his word—that at thirty he would turn his back on such a life as most men dream of and few achieve.

But he dressed and, putting his resolve away among his secrets, he went down smiling to breakfast with his family.

13

THE trademark introduction to some newsreels shows simultaneous shots of a bursting wave, a ballet, an express train rushing at you, a high dive, a football scrimmage, and other unrelated action. An account of Albert Schweitzer's life in the years following his Whitsunday resolve would need some such device to picture the several careers he was pursuing at the same time.

There is a room at the University of Strasbourg that looks out on a tree-lined, wall-enclosed garden where he lived and "conversed with the trees" even while he worked. For several years the floor of the room was cluttered with towering piles of books, each pile representing the material for a chapter of the book he was writing, *The Quest of the Historical Jesus*.

When the book was published, leading authorities agreed that it was "the most creative reconstruction of the life of Jesus that has ever been or, in all probability, that can ever be made from the records available."

At the same time Schweitzer was engaged in a life-saving campaign for the preservation of old church organs, lovingly built by hand, modest in volume but mellow in tone, that were in danger of being discarded for the giant, modern, factory-built instruments such as one hears in "motion picture cathedrals."

"Many a journey have I undertaken . . . and I have written letters by the hundreds, to bishops, deans, presidents of consistories, mayors, church committees, church elders and organists to try to convince them that they should restore their fine old instruments instead of replacing them with new ones."

He was also studying for his degree of Doctor of Philosophy, which he received when he was twenty-four.

Meanwhile he made flying visits to Paris, where he studied at the Sorbonne, took lessons on the piano and the organ, and was one of a small group to organize the Paris Bach Society. He considered French organs superior to the new German instruments, and said so in Germany, and in turn he played the German composer, Bach, to the French. It was his way of trying to bring the cultures of the two countries together, to offset the bitter memories of past wars and to prevent another.

And he was deep in the study of religions and received his degree in theology at the age of twenty-four. With it came an appointment to preach at the St. Nicholas Church in Strasbourg. "I felt it was something wonderful that I was allowed to address a congregation every Sunday about the deepest questions in life."

But some of the congregation complained that he cut his sermons short, and he was called before the "Inspector in Spiritual Matters" to defend himself against their charge. Schweitzer's defense was that he was "only a poor curate who stopped speaking when I had nothing more to say." He was dismissed with a mild reprimand and told that he was "not to preach for less than twenty minutes."

Schweitzer never did change in that respect, but it did not seem to hurt his career, for in the following year he was provisionally appointed Principal of the Theological College of St. Thomas, and two years later the appointment was made permanent.

It was a high post for a young man still in his twenties, but the university faculty were not the only ones who considered Schweitzer ready for it. Clergy from all over Alsace joined in recommending him for the post.

With it went the charge of a famous old library, a dignified official residence, a generous salary, and lifetime economic security.

All along he was working on the "little essay" on Bach, which developed into a long book. He wrote it first in French, and it was published in that language. So much demand for it came from Germany that he was asked to translate it. He tried to do it, but he found that the rhythms of the French language did not go well in German. Whereupon he rewrote the book completely.

He was often called to give organ recitals all over Germany, England, and Spain. He prepared his sermons on the train trips. He always gave a day to preparation for every concert, rehearsing on the organ to become acquainted with its individuality. He gave many a concert without any sleep between rehearsal and performance.

Meanwhile he was searching for the field in which he could fulfill his Whitsunday pledge. He had already been working with a group of fellow students, visiting families who were in need. This involved begging funds from purse-proud rich, something that was agony for Schweitzer, but he did it.

But to offset the grim side of their work the group saw to it that they also had a gay time of it. They made their visits on bicycles, then rode off through the Alsatian countryside for the joy of it. Cottagers came to their doors as they passed, attracted by their singing. They sang centuries-old student songs, some in Latin, and the latest popular hits, peasant songs, and songs composed by masters of music.

They danced, too, Alsatian dances, Vienna waltzes, and dances to the new and infectious music of America.

And there was laughter. The boy whom his teacher had called Isaac, "the laugher," was now a young man whose laughter came from a great chest, a rich mind, and a vibrant compassionate, nature.

Their talk was rich with the culture of centuries, exciting with fresh points of view, daring with prophecy, and colorful with young dreams.

Then, when they were in the mood and a church happened to be handy, they had Schweitzer play the organ.

Genius in the Jungle

One of the group was the daughter of a distinguished Jew, Professor Harry Bresslau, head of the department of history at the university. Helene Bresslau was studying pedagogics and sociology.

One day after hearing Schweitzer lecture she pointed out to him that there were French sentence forms in his German. He had already met with this problem in his other works, and he asked her to look at the drafts of some of his forthcoming lectures. She did, and he found her comments constructive.

He in turn wrote pamphlets for her in connection with some of the social work she was doing.

They found an increasing number of interests in common. Finally she told him what others did not know. She was being urged to take up teaching at the university. It was an alluring career, and she would remain in it until she was twenty-six. After that she would look about for some field of social work where human needs were more desperate.

He told her of his own program.

Thereafter it became increasingly clear that their lives were to be together.

Meanwhile Schweitzer was nearing his thirtieth birthday, and yet he had not found his lifework.

He had tried to find it in work with poor children, vagrants, and other jobless. But these were handled best by organizations, whereas he wanted to work not as a cog in a complex machine but as an individual, with a maximum of personal responsibility.

When an orphanage burned down he offered to take

in several children, but there he encountered the rigid
official passion for red tape and routine, and his offer
was rejected. So were several others of the kind.

But he kept searching, restricting himself, under-
standably enough, to work in Europe.

Then one morning, shortly before his birthday, someone laid a pamphlet on his desk, which he did not see
until evening. "In the very act of putting it aside so
that I might go on with my work," he wrote afterward,
"I mechanically opened it."

It was the monthly report of the Paris Missionary
Society, and it complained of a lack of missionaries and
doctors in the French colony of Gabon, in Equatorial
Africa.

Schweitzer had heard his father speak of the desperate plight there, of what he called "the most neglected
people on the face of the earth." In the Alsatian city of
Colmar Schweitzer had often pondered the sculptor's
version of one of them. It is the work of Bartholdi,
whose Statue of Liberty stands in New York harbor.
It is in stone, the head of a young Negro, physically
powerful and dignified, but pathetic with the look of
a bewildered soul in a hostile world. The stories that
Schweitzer had heard from his father of the needs of
the natives of the Gabon, together with the Bartholdi
figure, had made their impression on Schweitzer, but
until that time had not yet combined as a personal call
to him.

Now he read the article with its appeal for more
workers and its hope that the words "would meet the

eyes of men and women who can reply simply to the Master's call with, 'Lord, I am coming!' "

Schweitzer finished reading and put the magazine aside. "My search was over," he wrote.

Helene Bresslau was the only one to whom he confided that he had decided to spend the next eight years in the study of medicine, and that then he would go to the Gabon to cure the sick there.

She said she would wait for him to complete his course, then she would go with him.

He reminded her of the sacrifices this would mean for her, but said nothing of what it would mean to him, to give up music, security, teaching, preaching, and all the other riches of his life in Europe.

And he pointed out the hardships that would be hers in the Gabon. It was known as "the most unhealthful spot on earth." Only forty miles from the equator, it had a killing climate: a deadly sun and only two seasons, torrential rain and a dry season with the heat of a steam room. Everything disintegrated in the dank heat there, clothing, furniture, even buildings. What the climate did not destroy, termites and a host of voracious insects did. It was a country where cattle could not be raised because of the tsetse fly, carrier of sleeping sickness to beast and man. It was inhabited by the most primitive tribes on earth, most of them cannibals. They were afflicted with some of the worst diseases the whites could contribute, and they had a whole host of their own: raging, highly contagious fevers, virulent dysentery that laid low whole communities, heart ailments, skin diseases that ate deep into the tissues, limbs swollen to elephantine size, leprosy, insanity. And famine swept often over the land.

Did he have the right, he demanded, to expose her to such a malignant world?

She thought it all over seriously, then she smiled.

"I will take a training course in nursing," she said. "Then you won't be able to get along without me."

14

A FEW days later Schweitzer thrust a batch of letters into a mailbox. Some of them broke the news of his decision to family and friends. Others were withdrawals from a host of activities, and included his resignation as Principal of the Theological College of St. Thomas, with its lifelong security of income and its stately residence. As a medical student, he wrote, he would have no time to do anything else.

Genius in the Jungle

He had expected protests, but not the storm that broke.

Friends who had confided intimately in him reproached him for keeping them ignorant of so drastic a change in his own life.

Others even had unflattering theories as to why he was doing this: he was disappointed with his slow progress in the world. He did not bother answering this until much later in one of his books. "There was not the least ground for saying this, since even as a young man I was fortunate enough to get such recognition as others get only after long years of struggle." He laughed at himself and agreed heartily with those who called him a crackpot.

There were those who quoted the Bible at him, about the man to whom God had given a talent to use but who buried it instead.

Others asked him why he should waste years in studying medicine. "You're an ordained preacher already. Why not go there and simply preach?"

"Because I want to help with more than words."

He had a difficult time with a brilliant French woman. "You want to help medically?" she said. "Splendid! Stay in Europe, give lectures and recitals, write books that will bring you royalties, and you will make enough money to send twenty doctors out there, instead of just yourself."

He tried to argue that he had to be on the scene himself.

"Nonsense!" she retorted. "With enough money you

can hire just as competent executives, no matter how good you are."

She had the best of the argument, but she changed nothing.

His friend and teacher, Widor, scolded him. "You're like some general whose brains are needed more than his body, but who takes a rifle and exposes himself needlessly on the firing line."

The other members of the Paris Bach Society were even more impatient with Schweitzer. They were men of music, and to them giving up a great gift for music was as criminal as if a painter were to sacrifice his eyesight.

"At least take along an organ with you," they insisted. "We'll gladly give you one."

He pointed out that the last lap of his voyage would be in native canoes of hollowed tree trunks that were not designed to transport organs.

"Then we'll get you a small piano."

He told them that the climate and insects would rot its insides in no time.

But they paid no attention and went ahead with plans of their own.

His university colleagues objected also. "Service? Of course. But you teach. Isn't that service, too?"

He pointed out that there were others who could take his place in Europe but that there was not a doctor for hundreds of miles around in the Gabon.

He found that hardest of all was to dispel the worries of his family. His parents knew all about the Gabon country, and he could offer them no assurance that their fears for him were groundless.

He was glad when his medical course began.

First-year students at the Strasbourg University were amazed to see the recent head of one of its colleges sitting among them, a beginner like themselves.

He threw himself into his studies and found himself "intoxicated with delight" in dealing at last with a world of concrete facts, anatomy, chemistry, physiology, physics, and other sciences, after so many years of philosophical abstractions.

A medical course anywhere is a full-time program, and Schweitzer's was no exception.

But calls still came to him to come and save this or that old organ from destruction. After the many years he had put in trying to save them, he found he could not refuse these appeals for help. So he took time off, studying on trains and giving up sleep to make up for the time lost in classes.

He still had his book on Bach to finish. He worked at that, too.

He was still preaching at the Church of St. Nicholas. "Preaching was a necessity of my being." That meant time out for sermons and their preparation, and he gave them all the care he had devoted to them when they were his chief preoccupation.

He still had concerts to give. So he traveled to Paris, Barcelona, and to other cities, often spending whole nights, as before, in rehearsing on the organ he was to play the next day.

Albert Schweitzer

It was inevitable, therefore, that by the end of the third year at the medical school he found himself in "the worst crisis of exhaustion that I can recall at any time in my whole life."

By that time a little sleep was even worse than none at all, as so often happens when one has overdrawn on one's reserves. He had to have something that would rest him more than sleep. At such times, when it would seem that he could not take any more, and if the Church of St. Nicholas were deserted, he would climb to the organ loft and play.

Helene Bresslau would be listening somewhere below. Or she would sit by his side at the console and pull out the stops he indicated, so that in effect they would be playing as one.

And somehow he got through with his course by October, 1911, though there was still a state medical examination to take. There was a fee to pay, and he had to earn the money for it by performing at a musical festival in Paris. Those who heard him did not in the least suspect that he was in a fog of utter exhaustion.

On the morning of December seventeenth, after his last examination, he rose stiffly, and almost literally staggered out into a dark winter night. "I could not grasp the fact that the terrible strain of my medical course was behind me. Again and again I had to assure myself that I was really awake, and not dreaming. The voice of a friend who was walking with me seemed to come from some distant sphere. . . ."

Genius in the Jungle

He had a year to put in as a hospital intern.

He put in full time there, too, but also busied himself with the thousand and one details of preparation for Africa.

He had resigned his post at St. Nicholas Church. "I avoided as far as possible going past either St. Nicholas or the university. The sight of the places where I had carried on my work, and which I could never resume, was too painful for me."

After his year at the hospital he spent several months in Paris studying tropical medicine.

Then followed rounds of soliciting funds to build and run a hospital in the Gabon. Some friends gave gladly. In others he saw a change of manner when they learned that for the first time in their experience Albert Schweitzer was asking for help instead of giving it. On the other hand, he was touched by the readiness with which a group of German professors contributed to what, after all, was to be of benefit in a French colony. For at this time there was saber-rattling in Berlin and a cry for war against the French, and in France there was angry talk of revenge against their old foes, the Germans.

To the contributions he received he added whatever he could make at several recitals and concerts, until he had the equivalent of $5,000, enough to assure his work in Africa for two years.

He married Helene Bresslau on June 18, 1912.

A new experience followed. "Until then I had been engaged only in intellectual work. But now I had to make lists of things to do, to go shopping for days on end, to check accounts and deliveries, prepare lists for custom-house examinations, and other endless details." The man to whom "time was a precious gift" had to devote it now to countless items such as drugs, bandages, surgical instruments, and even the kitchenware the Schweitzers would need in their housekeeping.

At last, however, seventy packing cases of supplies were boxed and sent to Bordeaux, the Schweitzers' port of departure.

But he kept one heavy case to take along with them, two thousand francs in gold coin.

His wife asked him why, since paper money was so much easier to carry.

Gravely he told her.

In towering mountains on whose slopes snow and ice have been piling there comes a time when so much as a man's shout and its echo can let loose an avalanche. For years Russia, France, and Great Britain, on the one hand, and Germany and Austro-Hungary, on the other, had been piling up armament and racing to build up armies and navies. It would take very little to let loose such a war as the world had never known.

Schweitzer prayed that it would not happen, but if war did come he was determined nevertheless to build his hospital. And since paper money would be almost worthless in the event of war, he was taking gold instead.

So that, while along with the rest of the world he hoped for the best, he was prepared for the worst.

15

"THE church bells in my native Alsatian village had just stopped ringing on the afternoon of Good Friday 1913," Schweitzer wrote, "when the train on which my wife and I were to leave came around the corner of the woods. We boarded it, and our journey to Africa began. We waved our farewells from the platform of the last car, and for the last time I saw the spire of the church among the trees. When should we see it again? . . . When next day the Strasbourg Cathedral too sank from sight we seemed to be already in a foreign land."

The Schweitzers stopped off at Paris to hear Widor play.

After the music the other members of the Paris Bach Society took Schweitzer to see an enormous packing case, which they said would follow him to Africa.

It was an upright piano, zinc lined, with specially built pedals such as organs have.

At two that afternoon the Schweitzers left for Bordeaux.

Albert Schweitzer

Two days later they were aboard the small steamer *Europe*, of shallow hull, since it had to navigate an African river to reach its final port of call. Even in the quiet waters off the shore of France the boat rolled badly. In the Bay of Biscay a storm hit it.

Schweitzer had not thought to fasten his two cabin trunks. In the night they began chasing each other, and in trying to corner them Schweitzer almost had his leg crushed. He had to scramble to safety in his berth, and it was not until the morning that a steward managed to capture the trunks and tie them fast.

The storm lasted three days.

Then it calmed down and the sun came out. The Schweitzers were about to bask in it, when a fellow passenger warned them against it. "From now on you must regard the sun as your enemy, even at sunrise, sunset, and cloudy days. So never neglect to wear your sun helmets."

At Dakar, the Schweitzers set foot for the first time in Africa and went ashore for a visit. The city lies along a steep slope, and Schweitzer saw a horse trying to pull a cart heavily loaded with lumber up one of the steepest streets. It became stuck in a bit of bad road and could not move another step. Its drivers tried to mend matters with their clubs and yells of rage. Schweitzer stood it as long as he could, then rushed over, made the drivers dismount and help him push, until the horse could pick up the struggle.

A fellow passenger who was watching told Schweitzer, "If that's the way you feel about the treatment of animals, you had better turn back. You'll find Africa full of that kind of thing."

At port after port along the coast men and women left the ship, and their fellow passengers called, "Good health to you!" It was more than a conventional formula of farewell. It was what you wished anyone who was bound for the most unhealthful climate in the world.

Early one morning the Schweitzers transferred from the *Europe* to a river boat, the *Alembe*. They had entered the Ogowé, the principal water highway of the region.

"Water and primeval forest," Schweitzer wrote. "We seemed to be dreaming. . . . You cannot tell where water ends and land begins, it is so mirrorlike. . . . A mighty tangle of roots, covered with lianas, projects into the river. Palms and clumps of palms, towering high . . . the rotting trunks of dead giants. . . . Everywhere the water mirror sparkles blindingly. . . . At every bend new tributaries of the river show. . . . A heron flaps heavily upward and settles on a dead tree trunk . . . little blue birds skim over the water, and high in the air a pair of ospreys circle. . . . Then—yes, there can be no mistake!—from a palm something hangs down and swings, monkeys. . . . We are really in Africa . . ."

It was an attempt to see beauty, one way of looking at Africa, perhaps the wisest for one on the threshold of a life there.

But they passed the ruins of abandoned huts, their

roofs rotted by time and the weather. A French trader said pensively, "When I was here fifteen years ago these villages were all flourishing."

"What has happened to them?" Schweitzer asked.

The Frenchman shrugged his shoulders. "*L'alcohol*," he said.

Schweitzer thought of the centuries of slave trade that had been depopulating this country. Now alcohol was doing it.

Then, as though these were not enough infliction on the land, a powerful tribe of cannibals, the Pahouins, had moved into the Gabon. The whites of the region, protected as they were by empire, were safe from them, but not the natives living in the jungles many miles from the nearest police post.

The very air one breathed on the Ogowé was oppressive. On the ocean, even when the *Europe* was crossing the equator, there was life in the air. Now on the *Alembe* a steaming medium blanketed the body, brought the sweat pouring, and made the feel of one's very flesh and clothes almost a slimy indignity.

"Now the forest is a gigantic wall . . . from which there streams a heat that is almost unendurable."

Late the following afternoon the Schweitzers left the *Alembe* at a landing still an hour away from their destination. No one was there to meet them. Then, just as the Schweitzers were beginning to wonder, a dugout canoe paddled by native boys came shooting around the stern of the steamer, the winner of a race against another canoe. There was a white man in each, teachers at the mission to which the Schweitzers were going.

It developed that the race was to see which canoe was to have the Schweitzers as passengers. The dugouts were flat and narrow, the boys stood as they paddled, and it seemed to the Schweitzers when they got in one of them that at any moment they would have to finish their voyage by swimming.

But after an hour of suspense the Schweitzers relaxed. Then, on a branch off the main stream, they saw three hills topped by several white buildings, the windows blazing with the setting sun.

They were the buildings of a Paris Missionary Society School, on whose grounds Schweitzer had been given some land for his hospital. One building awaited them as their home, and they had been promised another would be ready for use as a clinic.

The Schweitzers were welcomed at the landing by the white workers at the mission and escorted to the house that was to be their home in Africa. Supported by some forty iron pillars that kept it twenty inches above the ground was a four-room house surrounded by a veranda. Children had decorated it with palms and flowers in honor of their coming.

The Schweitzers had dinner with Monsieur and Madame Christol. There were decorations of glowing paper lanterns and the children sang songs in French with verses composed for the occasion.

Then the Schweitzers were surrounded by a squad of lantern bearers as an honor guard and accompanied to their home.

Albert Schweitzer

When they were alone the Schweitzers looked out of the windows at the night that had fallen with the swiftness that so surprises newcomers to the tropics. There was no gracious, restful interval of twilight, only the blaze of sunset and almost sudden darkness.

Schweitzer lit a kerosene lamp. The doors and the windows had been well-provided with screens to keep out insects. But the room was swarming with flying cockroaches, which they had to battle. "Then came an ugly shadow creeping down the wall . . . a huge spider much larger than any I have ever seen in Europe." It had to be dispatched.

It was not alone the oppressive heat and the clamminess of the night that later kept him awake.

Somewhere in the jungle a dim drum was throbbing until it set up a throbbing in his nerves, and he determined angrily to see to it that when there were patients at the hospital those drums would stop after a given hour.

Whether the drum was for mourning or for some other ceremonial, it sounded troubling and at the same time troubled in itself, a fit voice for the uneasy life along the Ogowé. For every fear that a cannibal aroused in others, even he was haunted by fears of his own, real and imaginary; and the one has as much awful power over the primitive mind as the other. Schweitzer knew he would have to contend with insanity at his hospital.

He has not recorded his thoughts as he lay awake on his first night there. But he knew what a savage, many-sided struggle for survival was going on in the jungle behind the house. Man against man. Man against beast. Beast against beast. Mere insects carried death in their stings, and when their armies were on the march they devoured everything in their way. Even the jungle greenery was a massive, writhing, life-and-death struggle between parasites coiled about a host, sucking its life sap, and in turn trying to fight off other parasites doing the same to them.

And Schweitzer must have heard some of the sounds of the jungle night. Even the creatures that dared to fall asleep seemed to have uneasy dreams, and there were the chattering terrors of pursued animals and the outcry of some small creature that had been pounced upon and knew it was the end.

There may have come to him then a thought of Alsace, where all that might break in on the night would be the sleepy sound of treetops, or the cool liquid notes of a nightingale, and even they would seem to be trying to atone for the possibility that someone had been awakened.

If any such thought came to him it is certain that he quickly thrust it out of his mind.

part two

16

NEXT morning at six the Schweitzers heard a bell at
the mission and the voices of children singing a hymn.
The sun was already burning, and the day was oppressive.

Before his coming Schweitzer had been promised
that by the time he arrived there would be a building
of corrugated iron ready as the first unit of his hospital-
to-be. The Schweitzers hurried through their breakfast,
eager for their first glimpse of it.

To their dismay they found none.

The promise had been made in good faith, but the
lumbering season was on, and every available worker

was busy elsewhere, cutting down rosewood, mahogany, and other woods of the region for which there was increasing demand abroad.

It meant that the Schweitzers would have to start almost as primitively as Robinson Crusoe on his desert island, outdoors, with their bare hands and ingenuity, getting along with makeshifts. Had it been, like Crusoe's, only a problem of mere shelter and survival for themselves, the Schweitzers might have responded with zest to such a challenge.

But in medicine mere makeshifts may mean death, and there was no zest in the Schweitzers as they cast about to see what to do first.

They saw a wreck of a shack, and they looked in. It had housed chickens until it had become uninhabitable. The roof was rotted through. The walls had been originally whitewashed but were now indescribably filthy and bristling with mold and lichen. The earth floor was crusted with refuse. The sun beat down through the holes in the once-thatched roof more fiercely than outdoors, as though through focusing lenses.

But the Schweitzers borrowed brooms, a brush, and a pail of whitewash. They spent hours sweeping and cleaning, and Schweitzer covered the worst of the dirty walls with whitewash.

The mission gave them a camp cot, and this was to be the operating table in the "surgery."

Schweitzer had sent word before him that until the arrival of his seventy cases of supplies, on their way by slow boat, he wanted no patients except those who were in extreme need.

Now he saw canoes crowded with natives converging on the mission landing. When they had disembarked and began toiling uphill, he saw that some were limping and others were being carried.

The Schweitzers soon found themselves surrounded by sick natives, their friends, and their families. Of the babble in their ears they could not understand a word, though what they saw in many of the faces needed little translating.

Schweitzer had been promised an interpreter, N'Zeng, a Pahouin who had made remarkable progress from cannibalism to teaching at one of the missions, all in a few years. But now he was back in his native village sixty miles away involved in some property dispute, and it would be some time before he would be back.

Several of the natives around Schweitzer knew a few words of French, and he had to depend upon them and sign language for diagnosis and treatment.

He saw that a number of the natives had contagious diseases, and he had them stand apart from the others. But he treated them all outdoors in front of the hen house, under the burning sun.

Mrs. Schweitzer had brought out the kit of drugs, bandages, and instruments that they had taken with them on the voyage for personal use and emergencies. Side by side they worked all day, their eyes smarting

Albert Schweitzer

from the sun in spite of their helmets, their bodies drenched in sweat.

They had to stop when it turned dark. Not only was it hard to see, but mosquitoes were out, and in the Gabon they are more than a nuisance. For their sting carries the feared malaria, and sometimes even yellow fever.

The sun alone had been exhausting to the Schweitzers, and they had worked all day continuously and at high tension. But when Schweitzer lay in bed that night he had other things to think about.

In the Whitsunday morning reflections that had brought him here he had imagined bodies that had never known well-being, that were little more than carriers of sickness and of pain. Now he knew that those images were pale in the light of what he had seen this day.

He had met disease and pain, of course, throughout his medical course and as an intern. But close at hand there had been everything that medical science had developed in the way of relief and cure, the latest drugs, hospital appliances, radium, and all the paraphernalia necessary for the most delicate surgical operations.

Now he had to endure the thought of men and women dying on his hands for lack of what he knew could save them.

In his year of military service his body and his mind had lightheartedly carried on their separate activities at the same time. An onlooker would have said that on this, Schweitzer's first day in Africa, his whole mind and body were busy exclusively with treating his patients. But almost consciously throughout the day part of him was somewhere on the Atlantic trying to hurry the slow boat carrying his supplies.

In bed now, free of externals, his mind was on that boat. It was so slow . . . and many of his patients were going so fast . . .

What could he do? The answer was clear and emphatic. He could and must shut the whole day out of his mind and go to sleep. Otherwise he was being a bad doctor.

"Unfortunately, I am one of those medical men," he wrote later, "who lack the robust temperament so necessary in our calling. So I am consumed with unceasing anxiety about the condition of my critically ill patients. I have tried to acquire that equanimity which makes it possible for a doctor to husband his nervous and spiritual energy. But I have tried in vain."

17

DURING the next ten days, work at the "hospital" became a nightmare to the Schweitzers. The few drugs they had brought along had given out, and more and more patients kept coming. It was partly due to the witch doctors, who never took a case they could not cure. The hopeless ones were brought to Schweitzer.

Even with his limited means he managed to save some. Others he could not.

To add to the nightmare the natives refused to touch bodies for burial, and Schweitzer had to take spade in hand and help dig graves.

But one night he heard the first welcome sound in many a dark hour, the whistle of the steamer telling him his supplies were arriving.

In the morning, however, he learned that the captain of the steamer had refused to risk his craft in the shallow waters that led to the mission landing, and Schweitzer's seventy cases of supplies and the gift of the Paris Bach Society, the zinc-lined piano, had been put ashore some miles away.

Genius in the Jungle

Fortunately, two of the men at the mission were able to round up ten laborers with canoes and went to get the cargo. Unwilling to leave his work, Schweitzer waited at the mission. He could count on the safe arrival of the supplies, but he hated to think of the piano riding a dugout.

To his great delight there it was, along with the boxes, safe on board a canoe that had once been so gigantic a tree trunk that the craft could have carried five pianos.

Almost every adult and schoolboy at the mission helped to carry the cases up the hill. Even then, it took them three whole days. The problem had been where to store the contents of the seventy cases, not to mention the piano. But here again one of the missionaries helped, providing the planks and building shelves in the Schweitzers' home, which now became a supply room as well.

The piano dwarfed the living room.

With ample medical supplies the Schweitzers took heart. Mrs. Schweitzer assumed charge of the surgical instruments and the anesthetics. Schweitzer was ready to perform his first major surgical operation.

And, riding the tide of luck, came Joseph Azvawami. His tribe, the Galoas, had occupied the whole region before the Pahouins had come. Now the two tribes were neighbors, and the mission was on the borderline between their territories.

Schweitzer did wonders in curing Joseph, and the

patient stayed on to help him. In that Robinson Crusoe setting Joseph became Schweitzer's man Friday.

His lean and sensitive face shone with intelligence and good will. He had worked for French traders, spoke the language, was a good cook, and became an excellent interpreter. He even learned to take case histories of the patients, thereby saving Schweitzer much time. Joseph's reports, however, had a distinctive touch. He was more familiar with the names of cuts of meat for the table than with anatomical terms, and he would report that "this man's right leg of mutton hurts him," and "that woman has a pain in her upper left cutlet."

Schweitzer organized a system of recording clinical histories. Each patient was given a piece of cardboard which he wore suspended from his neck on a string of fiber. The tag bore a number, and on a patient's return visit the number told Schweitzer where to look for his or her previous history in the big book Schweitzer kept.

The patients ignored many of Schweitzer's instructions, but they always wore their tags. They did it not because it helped Schweitzer but because they took the tags to be amulets that would protect them from further illness.

Every day there were more and more of these amulets along the Ogowé, but it seemed to make no difference in the predominance there of disease and its concomitant, pain.

To a native, pain was a worm, and for him it was no mere figure of speech. When asked to describe his

Genius in the Jungle

symptoms, he would say that the Worm had entered his leg, or his head, and would the doctor, please, please drive the Worm out! When Schweitzer quieted a colic the patient would report joyfully that the Worm had been driven out of his body.

Pain was so prevalent along the Ogowé that there were few who had not witnessed at one time or another some man rolling on the ground screaming in agony. Most often it was due to strangulated hernia.

The first major operation that Schweitzer performed in the "surgery" was on one of these sufferers, who had been brought over a hundred miles, in agony all the way.

Schweitzer wrote: "When the poor moaning creature came, I laid my hand on his forehead and said, 'Don't be afraid. You will go to sleep, and when you wake up you will feel no more pain.' He was given an injection of omnipon; my wife was called, and with Joseph's help everything was made ready for the operation. . . . The operation was over, and in the dimly lighted interior I watched the man's awakening. Scarcely had he recovered consciousness when he stared about him and cried out again and again. 'I've no more pain! I've no more pain!' His hand felt for mine and would not let go. . . . The African sun shone in through the coffee bushes, as we, black and white, side by side, felt that we knew by experience the meaning of the words, 'And all ye are brethren.' "

With anodynes and anesthetics Schweitzer was now able to mitigate the tyranny of that pain which he called "a more terrible lord over man than death himself." What overwhelmed him was the prevalence of that which neither anesthetic nor anodyne could deaden, the fears that shattered many minds along the Ogowé.

When on that Whitsunday morning Schweitzer had promised himself some day to help men who lived in darkness and in fear he little dreamed in what a vast continent of darkness and of fear he would have to redeem his promise.

Its victims came to him often in the last stages of insanity, when he could neither cure them nor have the heart to send them back to the natives who had a simple way of dealing with the deranged. They either tied them hand and foot and threw them into the river or they drove them into the jungle.

Just as Schweitzer would have studied an epidemic at its source, he tried to understand the many types of terror that drive even the savage mind insane.

As though real life did not furnish fears enough, there was Fear's dreaded shadow, taboo, that has held sway over primitive minds from the beginning of time. On the Ogowé, even among cannibals, it was taboo to fill a hole with earth, to step over a procession of ants, to touch a chameleon—and there were a host of others.

And, as though general taboos were not affliction enough, there were the personal taboos for this or that man, woman, and child. One child was told that it was taboo to count his fingers. A boy was convinced that he must not be tapped on the right shoulder. A woman

86

Genius in the Jungle

for whom it was taboo to touch a broom swept her house with her bare hands. One native at Schweitzer's hospital believed that a blow on the head, no matter how light, would bring down on him untold horrors, so that whenever someone's hand came anywhere near his head he fainted.

At one of the mission schools a newcomer had brought the conviction with him that it would mean death for him to eat anything that had been in a pot in which plantains had been cooked. Some of his schoolmates, in mischief, told him that he had just eaten fish out of such a pot. The effect was terrifying, even for the others. The boy doubled up with cramps and died in agony.

Even more devastating than a taboo was the belief in the power of a curse. A native, for instance, whose daughter had refused to marry the man he had chosen for her, put a curse on her, telling her that if she married another man either she or her first-born would die at once. She married and bore a healthy baby, and rather than have it die she chose to die in his place, and did, for no reason that Schweitzer could ascertain except the power of autosuggestion. The infant was brought to him to be reared.

But the greatest source of terror for the native was the witch doctor. He was really the lord of life and death in the village. To incur his displeasure meant death, not because the tribe willed it but because the witch doctor had so many ways of bringing it about. He would pretend friendliness and use poison. Or he would convince some weakling that unless he killed a villager his own life was at stake.

Among the things the natives did not understand was sudden death due to a natural cause. There could be no other explanation for it except murder, either induced by a curse or through poison. In either case death had to be revenged by the dead man's kin.

One day a canoe came to the hospital with a dying man, and his family had also brought along a youth, obviously much against his will.

Schweitzer found the sick man far gone with an infection that could have been arrested in its early stages. As it was, the man was dying. Schweitzer told the family, and showed them what to do at the first sign of any other infection.

They were not listening to him. Their eyes were on the young man they had brought along, and he looked panic-stricken. Joseph told Schweitzer why. It seemed that back in their village, even before the sick man had caught the infection, the youth had had a dream in which he had killed the man, and foolishly he had told of his dream. When the man fell sick his family and friends decided that it had been no mere dream but a powerful curse. They had forced the young man to come along, so he would be there, should the curse turn out to be effective.

The sick man died, and the emotion his death aroused was not only a matter of grief. His family and friends surrounded the young man and tried to drag him to their canoe. He cried for help, and Schweitzer came running.

He threatened that if any harm came to the young man he would bring the guilty before the District Officer on a charge of murder, and he thought he had made an impression.

Just then there was a hurry call for him from the "surgery," and he had to leave. But the first moment he was free he hurried back to where he had left the terrified young man.

He was gone, and the others with him. A canoe was making speed away from the mission, and Schweitzer saw the young man in it, bound hand and foot. Schweitzer hurriedly organized a pursuit, but the canoe had had too good a start, and was soon out of sight.

To his dismay he found that no one knew in what village where to look for the party or how to rescue their prisoner. All they could tell Schweitzer was what awaited the young man.

Schweitzer thought of what an old Pahouin chief had said to him sadly, and he was not speaking of his cannibals: "Our country devours its own children."

He had been speaking of the many evils that afflict life along the Ogowé, but the subject had come up in connection with a number of very sick natives who had come to Schweitzer and whose symptoms had puzzled him as a doctor. The chief had cleared up the mystery for him.

It was the widespread use of poison in the villages between the Ogowé and the Congo rivers.

Albert Schweitzer

Witch doctors used mild doses of it to make villagers sick so that they would have to come to them to be "miraculously" cured. They used stronger doses of it on those who had incurred their displeasure. Joseph Azvawami knew all about it, too, but had not dared speak of it in his own village. He had seen too often what happened to those who had tried to expose a witch doctor. Not only did they die mysteriously and with spectacular agony, but their very deaths became "proofs" that the gods were on the side of the witch doctors.

And native used poison against native.

Sick at heart, that night Schweitzer tried to forget Africa for a while by working on one of his books. Suddenly his wife laid her hand on his shoulder and pointed.

The moon was little more than a crescent, but there was enough light to show shadows creeping out of the jungle toward the several patients who were sleeping in the "surgery."

Schweitzer uttered an exclamation of wrath. The shadows were cannibals on the prowl. Schweitzer seized a gun, flung open the door, and fired several shots into the air. The shadows streaked back into the jungle.

Schweitzer tried to get back to his writing, but he found that he could no longer get Africa out of his mind. Yet he knew that he must escape from that nightmare-ridden world, if only for an hour, or there would be no sleep for him that night.

Genius in the Jungle

But escape where? Europe?

News had been coming slowly and indirectly, but Schweitzer was holding his breath, expecting word any day now that the avalanche had broken loose in Europe. . . .

If it should come, Africa would seem a paradise by comparison. For, after all, murder there was only one-by-one, whereas in a world war the slaughter would be modern, machine-made, and on a scale of mass production that would make all other wars in history seem mercifully antiquated. . . .

Could civilized man survive the war? Were there enough drugs and bandages and doctors and nurses to bind up the many wounds? Even his own small share in that stupendous task would be taken away from him, for he and his wife were German subjects in a French colony. . . .

It all came closing in on him until the man who had always met his problems head-on found that for at least a breathing spell he simply had to turn away from it all.

There was only one escape for him that night. Schweitzer had not touched the piano that his friends of the Paris Bach Society had given him. It was not lack of time that had kept Schweitzer from it. If one must cut off a beloved past, it is best to make a clean cut of it, and Schweitzer had determined to let his fingers lose touch with music. Any reminder of their old skill would only bring pain without hope of relief. Now he felt that nothing of the past could bring such pain as did the present, and if music could help him forget it for the time being he was willing to pay the price.

He went to the piano, raised the lid, sat down and played.

For the first time since creation the jungle about him heard Bach performed by a master, and if Bach's music, as Schweitzer has said, is an act of worship, then there must have been something of prayer in the playing.

18

LAMBARÉNÉ, a village of several hundred houses, mostly native huts, lies across the river from the Paris Mission post and gave the place name to the mission and the grounds on which the "hospital" was located. The main house of the mission and the boys' school was on the hill farthest upstream; the Schweitzer home and the "surgery" were on the middle hill; and the girls' school and another building occupied the third.

The jungle wall was only sixty feet away and was a

hundred feet high, a barrier to any breeze that might have come, and in itself was the source of heat that seemed to come from a vast furnace.

No one dreamed of using the jungle paths for a stroll or for cooling shadow. There was no other place for a walk but the rectangle of cleared land on which the mission stood, a third of a mile long and only a third of that as wide. Everyone in the settlement knew the dimensions almost to a foot, much as a prisoner knows his cell.

"If we could only cut down a corner of the jungle which shuts in the lower end of the mission," Schweitzer wrote. "We might then get a bit of breeze from the river. But we have neither the money nor the men for such a project."

He had neither the money nor the men for projects he needed more vitally.

"My work is rendered all the harder by the fact that I can keep so few drugs in the hen house. For almost every patient I have to cross to my home, there to weigh out or to prepare the needed medicine, which is very fatiguing and wastes much time. When will the work on the iron building for the hospital be seriously begun? Will it be ready before the rainy season comes? What shall I do if it is not ready then? It is so hot in the hen house that it is impossible to work there, and the sun pours in through the roof. . . . More and more patients keep coming, but my supplies are giving out. Quinine, antipyrin, bromide of potassium, salol, and dermatol, they are almost gone. . . . It may be three, four months before I get any more from Europe. . . ."

His estimate of the time was a bit of evasion. If war did come, it would not be merely a matter of months before the supplies would come. . . .

That was his mood one day. The next day, refreshed perhaps by Bach or a night of sleep less broken than usual by calls from the "surgery," he wrote:

"Yet what are all these disagreeable things compared to the joy of being here, working, helping? However limited one's means, how much one can do! Just to see the relief and joy of those who have been treated, bandaged, and given rest after they had dragged their poor bleeding feet through the jungle, that in itself makes work here worthwhile. . . ."

Nevertheless, trifles that would not have troubled even a laboratory assistant in Europe became almost major problems for the head of the hospital in Lambaréné.

He had to give medicines, for instance, to discharged patients to take along. In Europe there would have been containers, paper envelopes, cardboard boxes. In the steaming climate of Lambaréné paper containers simply fell apart, and only bottles and cans would do. Schweitzer had only a limited number of them, and he would beg his patients to return them to him. But they remained in the native villages as prized possessions and ornaments. Every mail from Schweitzer to friends in Europe were begging letters, for bottles big and little and other durable containers. ". . . and please don't forget the corks for the bottles, and do send some test tubes and tin cans! How I look forward to the day when I can have enough of them!"

But they were trifles, after all, in comparison with his growing imperative need for more hospital space, grounds, and buildings. For that he would have to apply to the regional heads of the missionary organization that was about to have a conference at Samkita at the end of July.

He had no choice but to go there.

One misty morning before daybreak Schweitzer and two missionaries set out in a canoe manned by twelve natives. The canoe was also loaded with pineapples, to quench the thirst of passengers and crew, and with bunches of bananas for the crew's food supply. Schweitzer wished they had more substantial food for the hard paddling they would have to do, but the natives themselves seemed to worry little about it and were singing as they started out.

But their singing stopped abruptly when the first rays of the sun showed several dark shapes swimming in the river ahead of them, and the natives gave them wide berth. They were a herd of hippopotamuses, whose moods are unpredictable, and Schweitzer approved wholeheartedly of the detours they had to make even though it meant a delay in arriving at Samkita.

Sunrise brought out the tsetse flies, whose bite goes through the thickest cloth, but they shy away from bright colors, and Schweitzer and the others wore such colors for protection.

They reached Samkita by late afternoon, and at the

sight of new faces, white missionaries and their **Negro** colleagues, Schweitzer felt an almost forgotten pleasure.

The conference lasted a week.

"I felt it inspiring to be working with men who for years had renounced so much in order to devote themselves to the services of those who had so little," Schweitzer wrote.

He was among the speakers at the conference, and he had to touch on religion. A young Negro missionary, fresh from school and full of zeal, disagreed with some of his statements. He knew Schweitzer only as the doctor from Lambaréné, and was quite tolerant with him. "I disagree with Dr. Schweitzer," he said, "but then he can't know everything. After all, he is not a theologian."

The former head of the Theological School of the Strasbourg University did not contradict him.

The conference not only approved of Schweitzer's request for more ground and a new building but also contributed some of the cost of putting it up.

On his return to Lambaréné, Schweitzer managed to round up several laborers, "after a world of trouble," and the work of clearing the site for the new building began. But the laborers proved to be "magnificently lazy," and Schweitzer had to join the work gang, while the native foreman "lay in the shade and occasionally threw us an encouraging word."

Fortunately a lumber merchant came along and lent Schweitzer eight of his workers, at the high rate of pay they demanded. In two days the site was leveled, and Schweitzer took hope. But payday dashed it, for the laborers went to Lambaréné, spent the money on a roaring drunk, and Schweitzer and Joseph had to finish the clearing in their spare time and without help.

Then a hurry call came from a woman missionary who was desperately ill at a post far up the river, and Schweitzer had to go. The trip there and back took several days.

When his canoe neared the landing Schweitzer was startled by a change in the skyline on the middle hill.

The corrugated-iron building was up.

Two of the mission workers, together with Joseph and several of the natives who had come to the hospital with their sick, had combined to spring a surprise on the doctor.

Schweitzer rejoiced over it as though a palace had been presented him. There were two rooms, each thirteen feet square, and two smaller rooms under the projecting roof of thatch. The floors were cement. Along the walls were shelves of mahogany and rosewood, which along the Ogowé were cheaper than the cheapest lumber elsewhere.

The addition to the hospital set off a veritable outbreak of more feverish building. Schweitzer himself did the work of several men. Joseph performed heroic labors. Two of the missionaries, M. Kast, a Swiss, and Señor Ottman, an Argentine, who had already done much of the work on the corrugated-iron building, now helped with the others.

A small, new building served as a waiting room.

The corrugated-iron building became the surgery.

A neatly constructed hut became Joseph's private residence. Temporary shelters went up for the families and friends of the sick.

Finally one morning the walls and the roof of the sick ward itself went up.

In the morning Schweitzer summoned sixteen patients into the building that was as yet only a shell. With a pointed stick he marked out sixteen rectangles on the earthen floor with passages between them. Each patient lay down in a rectangle. Their families and friends were sent off with axes to bring in the makings of the beds.

Canoes scurried up and down the river and were back in a few hours with cut poles, masses of jungle vines strong as rope, and piles of dried grass.

At each corner of a rectangle short, stout posts were driven into the ground, every one of them with a forked top. They supported six-foot poles for the sides of the beds and shorter ones for the ends. The tough vines were strung tightly across and were so close together that they made a resilient spring for mattresses of dried grass.

Now the patients lay down on comfortable beds, with space under each for food and cooking utensils. By nightfall the problem was to keep the healthy from ousting the sick from the beds that proved so enticing.

But every improvement of the hospital became so publicized in the jungle that it brought all the more patients.

With their increase a new and vital problem arose.

Genius in the Jungle

The understanding had been that patients and their friends and families would bring their own food. That was the theory. What actually happened was that they seldom brought enough, especially when the patient had to stay longer than was expected.

The result was that quarrels arose among them when food shortages developed. Schweitzer was now called upon to act as judge and peacemaker, as well as doctor.

One day, for instance, a native helped himself to another's canoe at night, and went fishing. When he came back the next morning the owner of the canoe raised a commotion and demanded the fish as his. Schweitzer had to intervene.

He heard both sides, then decided.

"You are both in the right and also in the wrong," he said. "You, as owner of the canoe, are in the right because he should have asked permission to use it. Therefore, you are entitled to a third of his catch. But you are also in the wrong on two counts. You should have fastened your canoe with a padlock, as you have been shown. And you are guilty of laziness. There was good moonlight for fishing and you stayed in bed."

He turned to the other. "You were wrong in taking the canoe without permission, so you owe the owner a third of the fish. But you were right in making use of the moonlight to go fishing. Therefore, you are entitled to a third of what you caught. And the hospital is entitled to a third because it took place on our grounds, and you have taken some of the doctor's time in adjusting this dispute."

Albert Schweitzer

However just the verdict may have been, with its profit to the hospital, it did nothing to solve the growing and basic problem of food for all.

"Paradox though it may seem," Schweitzer wrote, "nowhere is it easier to starve than amidst the luxurious vegetation of the game-haunted forests of Equatorial Africa."

For, lavish though the region was with jungle growth, it was not generous with food for human beings. Practically all the citrus fruits, bananas, yams, potatoes, and other fruits and vegetables had been introduced along the Ogowé by whites. The natives had learned to grow bananas, plantains, and other foods, but cultivation has been crude and beset with difficulties. The banana rapidly exhausts the soil, and the natives have to clear the jungle for new plantations every few years. Elephant herds often raid them, and whatever they don't eat they destroy.

Rains often fail the natives, and drought brings famine.

Fishing is a fairly dependable source of supply, but in spite of the wealth of wild life in the jungles the hunting is not so good. Notwithstanding the fabled skill with bow and arrow that the primitive savage is supposed to have, it is sometimes more fable than fact; and, though many have learned to use guns in hunting, the weapons are often as poor as the natives' marksmanship. Then, too, after you have shot something high in the jungle growth you may find it almost impossible to get at it through the tangle.

Genius in the Jungle

All of which made it imperative for Schweitzer to develop an unfailing source of food for his hospital. He rounded up a work gang of natives and set them to clearing land for a plantation.

Just then another hurried call for him came from a distant post, and he had to take a canoe and a crew along to go there. He left word that the tract must be cleared, or nearly so, by the time he got back.

His crew and he took guns along, and the natives were looking forward to some good hunting.

But they complained throughout the trip.

"Nothing ever happens when we go with you," said their spokesman. "If we were with Mr. Calder [one of the missionaries], he would have shot some monkeys and birds. But you pass them by and never a shot!"

He pointed above their heads, at beautifully crested cranes, green and gold pippios, and other gorgeously plumaged food.

It was a cruel dilemma for the man who had never outgrown the boy on the hunting party in Alsace who could not get himself to shoot birds. And he was letting personal feelings stand in the way of food for his men.

He compromised. He shot no birds. But when a monkey showed high in the thick tangle of greenery, he fired. The body dropped through the branches but caught were it would be hard to get at. The natives tried but took so long that Schweitzer joined them.

They came back without the animal Schweitzer had shot, but in his arms was an infant monkey that had been left motherless.

Instead of adding to the food supply he had brought back one more mouth to feed.

When he got out of the canoe at Lambaréné Schweitzer was still pondering his dilemma and the problem set up by his unwillingness to destroy any living thing.

Just then he caught sight of a movement in the grass, a pair of beautifully colored but deadly coral snakes, with their newly hatched brood. Snakes along the Ogowé are everywhere—underfoot, in the greenery, and even drop into canoes from trees overhead. They range from the smallest of the species to the giant pythons and boa constrictors, and practically all are deadly.

Roaming in the grass near the coral snakes were several naked native children.

For some moments the artist in Schweitzer reveled in the sinister beauty of the parent snakes, and the instinctive, already exquisite grace of their young. Then he raised his gun and blasted parents and younglings into so much flying pulp.

He hurried to see what progress had been made on clearing the plantation.

Not a stroke of work had been done in his absence.

Every white at the mission was as overworked as Schweitzer, and the help they had given him in the past was at the expense of their own work. This time they had not been able to help him.

Nor had Joseph done anything about the plantation. He had taken Schweitzer's place to a remarkable extent, even performing complicated treatment of emergency patients. Though he could not read, he had memorized the looks of scores of labels on medicine bottles and had used their contents without a mistake.

Mrs. Schweitzer had not helped with the orchard. Her housework included not only her home but also the whole hospital. The laundry alone was a full-time job. In addition, she was everything from nurse to cook and surgical assistant, for Joseph had long been promoted out of the kitchen. With her husband away, in addition to all her other work, she had had to take on many of his tasks with the sick as well as with the others, from babies to the aged, with their many disputes and other personal problems.

But there in the shade, by the side of the work they were supposed to have done, lay the laborers and their foreman, taking their ease. Schweitzer came over and glared at them for a time, then the whole mission could hear his anger.

But the foreman rose and said quietly, "Do not shout at us so, Doctor, it is all your own fault. Stay here and we will work, but when you are at the hospital or away somewhere else, we are alone and do nothing."

He was faced by a condition that was as hard to change as the climate, since it was partly due to the climate.

That meant one more demand on him.

But how much more could he do? Could he even keep up what he had been doing? For he and his wife had been in Lambaréné over a year now, in a climate that was hard even on easygoing whites, and the Schweitzers had been anything but easygoing.

Schweitzer knew now that tropical anemia was developing in both his wife and himself, and in addition he had caught some infection that had better be seen to by a skilled surgeon before long.

Finally Schweitzer was forced to make a painful decision. He reduced the number of his patients to a minimum, sent the others away, left Joseph in charge, and set out for Cape Lopez with his wife, where they could get medical attention and some recuperation.

19

THE Schweitzers were sitting in the cabin of the river steamer, limp with heat and exhaustion, their eyes closed.

The boat had reached the mouth of the Ogowé, then made a sharp turn. Suddenly the Schweitzers were startled. They had forgotten the feel of ocean air. They opened their eyes in the breeze that came in, stared incredulously at each other, smiled like children who had been inexpressibly surprised by some marvelous gift, closed their eyes again, and let the heavenly freshness flow through their famished veins. Then they sank into the sweetest sleep, it seemed to them, that they had even known. When they awoke, the hollows about their eyes were lighter, their eyes themselves had lost their lackluster look, and their cheeks were tinged with the faint promise of returning health.

Schweitzer's infection got well of its own accord.

Meanwhile a Frenchman, whose wife had been cured at the Schweitzers' hospital, invited them to stay at his house at Cape Lopez. It was on a hill overlooking the ocean, and the Schweitzers spent whole days in armchairs on the porch, just looking at the Atlantic Ocean.

Then they went back to Lambaréné.

The whole mission and the few patients who were at the hospital were at the landing to welcome them. But Schweitzer saw a subtle uneasiness in the faces of the French workers, and he guessed the cause. The Schweitzers, although Alsatians, were, after all, German subjects, and war was imminent. There was not the least trace of personal feeling in this; on the contrary, war would not make the slightest difference in the high regard the mission felt for the Schweitzers; but word was sure to come from the governors of the colony, once the war broke out, declaring them to be enemy aliens.

Albert Schweitzer

Schweitzer was so recharged with energy that for the next two nights he went back to his old student trick of stretching a workday to twenty-four hours.

On the third day he sent Joseph with some medicine to give to the captain of the river steamer for delivery to a patient on the coast.

Joseph came back with the medicine and a note from the captain, and from the expression on his face Schweitzer knew that the worst had come.

The note read: "Europe is at war. I am instructed to put my steamer at the disposal of the authorities, so that I cannot say when the *Alembe* will go to Cape Lopez next."

And late that afternoon several armed natives arrived, acting under orders of the Gabon authorities, forbidding the Schweitzers all further contact with natives and whites.

As enemy aliens, the order read, Doctor and Mrs. Schweitzer were prisoners in the custody of the bearers of the order.

The bearers of the order did not look too happy about it. And as the afternoon wore on, their lives were made miserable by the natives who had been Schweitzer's patients.

Schweitzer finally had to rescue his guards from the abuse of the others. Then, looking almost as gaunt as when he had left Lambaréné as a sick man, he told his patients to go home and closed down the hospital.

20

JOSEPH stayed on, but otherwise the Schweitzers could not believe their eyes, so strange did it seem to see the hospital buildings and grounds empty and so unbelievable to find time heavy on their hands.

Schweitzer caught up on lost sleep, then resumed work on a book he had begun in Europe. It was an analysis of the mysticism of St. Paul. Schweitzer had written his book on Jesus; now he wanted to do another on the man who next to Jesus occupies the most important place in the history of Christianity.

It was restful at first to leave the present and go back two thousand years, to picture the influence of a great civilization, the Greek, on a superior mind and spirit, and to reflect on the nature of mysticism, faith, and a transcendent love of humanity.

It would have stayed restful for anyone else but Schweitzer, or even for him at a time less overwhelming. As it was, anything and everything brought him back brooding on the present.

He saw, for instance, an invasion of traveler ants. He

would have had to pay strict attention to them in any event and done something about them at once, but he became absorbed in the uncanny likeness of their behavior pattern to the armies on the march in Europe.

The ants marched six abreast in four parallel columns, in almost perfect military order, rapidly, but it would take their army thirty-six hours to pass a given point. That day they were converging on the little house where the Schweitzers kept hens.

The moment the ants came to a relatively clear space on the ground where an attack from enemy insects might be expected a swift change took place in the procession. The ants that carried their young on their backs kept marching. But there was a scurrying of warrior ants to each side of the line of march. Forming continuous walls on both sides, they turned their backs to the procession, "much like Cossacks when protecting the Czar," Schweitzer wrote. And with powerful jaws open and ready, they waited until the danger seemed to be over in that particular clearing, then rejoined the marchers.

When the army reached a cluster of huge spiders, regarded as edible by the ants, it looked as though a sudden command had been given. For in a twinkling the ground was a swarming mass of insects climbing after the spiders, who fled desperately up the trees, but in vain. Those that were overtaken on the way up were thrown down to the devouring masses below. Some spiders, in apparently insane terror, actually threw themselves to the ground, as though suicide were better than the nightmare of being overtaken.

Sounds of alarm came from the hen house. The vanguard of the army was already there. Unless stopped, they would swarm into the eyes, mouths, and nostrils of the fowls and would have picked the flesh clean to the bone had not Mrs. Schweitzer, alerted by her husband, taken a bugle from the wall and blown it in pre-arranged signal. Joseph and others came running with pails of water in which there was Lysol. It was poured over the invaders.

Now the warrior ants swarmed over the Schweitzers and the others, sinking their jaws into the flesh. Schweitzer counted fifty on one of his arms. Once a traveler ant bites, it cannot be brushed off, for the jaws remain in the flesh and have to be removed separately.

But the ants, unable to stand the fumes of the Lysol, were in retreat.

The battle had fully occupied Mrs. Schweitzer and the others, but though Schweitzer had been as active as the others, all that he could think of was the reality of which this had been only a reminder in miniature.

Gradually the watch over the Schweitzers was relaxed, the guards drifted away, and natives came to talk to Schweitzer, asking him about this incredible war that was going on. He found the questions hard to answer.

They asked, for instance, why Christians whose religion preached brotherly love should be engaged in world-wide war.

It was not long before ten among the white men of

the region who had been called to Europe were killed in action. Schweitzer's friend, the old cannibal chief, asked if it was true.

"Yes," Schweitzer said sadly.

"Will there be more killed?"

"I'm afraid so."

"Then why don't they have a good talk and stop the war? And they must be killing each other out of cruelty, since I am told that they do not eat their dead."

Schweitzer had no answer to that.

Then natives were drafted for service, some as laborers, others to fight. Some of the latter did not come back.

Schweitzer had gone to a river village to see some of the conscripted natives he knew who were embarking for the war. As the steamer drew away from the landing a wail arose among the native women near Schweitzer. Eventually, however, all but one of the women left.

"The crowd had dispersed," Schweitzer wrote, "but on the riverbank an old woman, whose son had been taken, sat weeping silently. I took her hand and tried to comfort her, but she went on crying as if she did not hear me."

Finally the man who had not wept in public since the day when he had been stung by a bee at the age of two now wept openly.

When he got home he knew that he could no longer take refuge in the remote theme of St. Paul. He had to face the present, as any medical man would have to face an epidemic and do something about it. Prisoner that he was, he could do little but think and write.

But diagnosis is a form of action, too, and Schweitzer had long been thinking about the causes of decay of modern civilization. Now it became an imperative task for him to bend all his mind and energies on the diagnosis of a sick humanity.

It did not take the actual outbreak of a world war to set him thinking about its coming. The war was only the violent and visible aspect of what he had been studying for many years.

"We are living today under the sign of the collapse of civilization," he now wrote, the first sentence of his new book. "The situation has not been produced by the war; the latter is only a manifestation of it. . . . It is clear now to everyone that the suicide of civilization is in progress. What yet remains of it is no longer safe. It is still standing, indeed, because as yet what is still left of it has not been exposed to the destruction that has overwhelmed the rest, but, like the rest, it is built on rubble, and the next landslide will very likely carry it away. . . . But what was it that preceded all this and has led to the loss of power in the innate forces that should have kept our civilization alive and healthy?"

It seemed to him that man was losing an inner guidance that even animals still possessed.

He was not thinking only in abstract terms. There came to his mind several instances of that guide to survival which animals still retained and man was losing.

There was the orphaned baby monkey he had

brought back from the hunt. There were already several grown monkeys making themselves at home on the hospital grounds. He gave them the orphan to bring up. "Many times it happened," he reported, "that the seemingly worst-tempered monkeys were the very ones who insisted most on assuming this sudden burden of foster parenthood."

He also told of a friend of his who used to throw crumbs to sparrows on the sidewalk in front of his favorite café table. One day he saw a sparrow that had been injured and therefore could not compete for the crumbs against the others. He was about to help it when he saw that the other sparrows, "apparently by mutual agreement, were not touching the crumbs that were nearest the injured bird."

He was fond of telling of another instance of the kind, of a flock of wild geese that was on its way south to escape the winter and had settled on a pond for a brief rest. A man managed to capture one of them, and out of idle curiosity clipped its wings to see what would happen. Would its companions go on without it? The goose tried in vain to follow when the others set off again. But they saw that he could not fly. Against all their instinct to keep going, the flock settled back on the pond again, waiting for days for their crippled companion to recover. He finally did and took wing. It was only then that the rest of the flock left with him.

What was it, Schweitzer pondered, in civilization that had decayed in man but still survived in animals?

His writing was interrupted by a native who came

with a message from the regional French administrator. The note was so unimportant that Schweitzer wondered why the administrator had taken the trouble to send it. Then he saw the messenger was badly ailing, and Schweitzer knew why he had been sent. It was the Frenchman's way of getting Schweitzer to do what had been officially forbidden him.

The messenger stayed down at Lambaréné until he was cured.

Many similar notes followed, until the hospital resumed its old look and activity.

Meanwhile, in Paris, Charles Widor and the other members of the Paris Bach Society had been plaguing French government officials on behalf of a supposedly enemy alien in the Gabon. The result was that one day an order came to the French head of the Gabon to allow the hospital at Lambaréné to function officially.

Schweitzer did not feel he had much to celebrate at Christmas, but he did set up a little potted palm as the tree and lit a few candles on it. When they were half burned, he snuffed them out.

"Why?" his wife asked.

"We may want the rest for next Christmas." he said. "I don't think there will be any fresh ones to be had."

Candles were not the only supply that the war had cut off.

In warehouses in Havre and Bordeaux there were cases of medical supplies waiting for ships to take them to Lambaréné and for seas to be cleared of submarines.

They kept on waiting.

The gold francs in Schweitzer's strongbox were nearly gone, and no other money was in sight. Schweitzer had to reduce the nominal salary he had been paying Joseph, until the day came when his faithful assistant could no longer support himself and his wife and sorrowfully bade good-by and went back to his village.

Not only drugs were giving out. Food was running short at Lambaréné, and still worse, all along the Ogowé. It became even scarce for the whites there. What few ships had managed to escape the German submarines brought supplies that were so much in demand that prices soared beyond the reach of most.

Cultivation fell off, so many natives had been called to war.

Food at the hospital became a daily increasing problem and heartache.

The only increase at Lambaréné was the number of those who came there to be cured.

Schweitzer did not need to have a concrete reminder, night and day, of insanity in the world, but it came to him nevertheless.

One night he was awakened by cries on the hospital grounds, and when he reached the scene he saw that an old woman had been brought there and was now tied to a tree. She was raving insanely. Her family was with her. He told them to untie her. They obeyed, but in great fear and, as it developed, with good reason for it. Schweitzer had been holding a lighted lamp, and the moment the woman was free she leaped at him and tried to snatch the lamp. The family fled, shrieking.

Genius in the Jungle

Schweitzer grasped her arm and made her sit down quietly. Eventually she even let him give her an injection of morphine and scopolamine. A little later she was quietly sleeping in an extemporized shelter.

But she made other nights hideous with her cries.

It all seemed of a piece, Schweitzer's well-nigh insoluble problem with her and his wrestling with the problem of the world at large.

He knew what ailed it, as well as he knew what ailed her. But what to do about insanity, individual and collective? It was only too easy to diagnose. Many others had already done it. There was the book by Oswald Spengler, *The Decline of the West*. It was an exhaustive analysis and prophecy of doom for white civilization, and was dominant in the minds of many.

But what good does it do a man to be told that he is doomed?

It went against Schweitzer's grain to accept the thought of ultimate defeat, and it was his duty as a doctor to go beyond the diagnosis even when it seemed that there was no hope for the patient. He must bend all his efforts toward finding and effecting a cure. . . .

What was the cure for western civilization? It had lost its bearings and must find its right course again. Its great gift of invention was flourishing as never before, but it was producing only still more effective devices for killing. It had had guidance enough from the great teachers of religion, but after thousands of years all that man had seemed to learn was to wage more and more devastating wars.

Albert Schweitzer

". . . I seemed to myself to be like a man who has to build a new and better boat to replace a rotten one in which he can no longer trust himself to the sea," he wrote, "and yet does not know how to begin.

"While in this mental condition I had to undertake a longish journey on the river. . . . The only means of conveyance was a small steamer towing an over-laden barge. . . . Slowly we crept upstream, laboriously feeling—it was the dry season—for the channels between the sandbanks. Lost in thought, I sat on the deck of the barge, struggling to find the elementary and universal conception of the ethical which I had not discovered in any philosophy. Sheet after sheet I covered with disconnected sentences, merely to keep myself concentrated on the problem. Late on the third day, at the very moment when, at sunset, we were making our way through a herd of hippopotamuses, there flashed upon my mind, unforeseen and unsought, the phrase, 'Reverence for Life.' The iron door had yielded: the path in the jungle had become visible . . ."

He had found the basic belief that not even the most skeptical and material-minded could deny.

Even the lowest conceivable form of life follows a basic drive not only to survive but also to grow, and its will to fulfill itself in life seems to be one with the vast universe within which it finds itself.

"I am life which wills to live, in the midst of life that wills to live . . ."

Schweitzer came back to Lambaréné and went to work furiously on his book, *The Decay and The Res-*

toration of Civilization that he planned as his contribution to a world in travail.

But the world seemed to be more interested in hampering him than in finding salvation.

For an order came through from France which even Schweitzer's devoted friends in Paris could not head off.

It instructed the authorities to round up all the "enemy aliens" in the Gabon and to ship them forthwith to prison in France for the duration of the war.

With native military guards standing over him, Schweitzer had to tell the sick and the insane woman to leave.

Their lamentations were still ringing in his ears long after the canoes were out of sight on the river and on the jungle trails.

Fortunately the steamer that was to take the Schweitzers away was several days late, and it gave them a chance to do what they could to protect the hospital buildings against the coming siege of time, jungle, and climate. There was no way, however, for them to protect the orchard and the vegetable garden that had cost so much time, money, and labor.

Then, just as the Schweitzers were in the midst of their packing, a screaming native was brought in the throes of strangulated hernia, and Schweitzer, assisted by his wife, had to operate on him.

It was just such agony that he had relieved by his first major operation at Lambaréné, and, now that he was leaving, it was also his last.

Albert Schweitzer

The Schweitzers boarded the river steamer under guard, but some of the French missionaries, defying rules of conduct toward prisoners of war, came down to bid them heartfelt farewells.

From the deck of the steamer they watched the receding scene of four and a half years of their labors.

Several days later, from the deck of the *Afrique* they saw the shores of the continent itself disappear.

part three

21

THIS time the ocean air brought no returning health to the Schweitzers. Africa had eaten into them too deeply, and they knew that they would be getting worse for a long time before they could hope for improvement.

They were under close guard throughout the whole trip, forbidden to talk to anyone but the steward who had been assigned to take care of their small cabin.

They were confined to their cabin except for strictly supervised exercise on deck. "Since writing was impossible," Schweitzer reported later, "I filled my time in learning by heart some of Bach's fugues and Widor's Sixth Organ Symphony."

He did it by using the top of his trunk as an imaginary organ console and pressing imaginary pedals on the cabin floor.

It was not energy that drove him to it. "The Alsatian Giant" to whom sleep had so often seemed unnecessary was now conscious only of increasing fatigue. Africa had got the better of his lowered resistance, and disease was burrowing deep into his system. His "organ playing" was an effort to keep from thinking of what lay ahead.

The *Afrique,* in time of peace, had been a spotless luxury steamer. Now that the war was on, it showed neglect everywhere—except in the Schweitzers' cabin. The steward, a Frenchman who had held himself otherwise aloof, kept it especially clean, served them their meals with fastidious care, and in every way gave them superior service.

When the boat sailed into Bordeaux harbor, Schweitzer thanked him, and ventured to ask why he had given him better service than other prisoners of war had received from him and the other stewards. He had even refused a tip from Schweitzer.

Now that the voyage was over the steward relaxed toward his war prisoners. "You may thank M. Gaucher," he said, "a former passenger and my good friend. 'Gaillard,' he said to me, 'it is likely that before long the doctor from Lambaréné may be one of your passengers. If so, for my sake, please treat him well. He saved my life at the hospital.'"

At Bordeaux the Schweitzers and the other prisoners

of war were quartered in temporary barracks that had been used for troops on the way out to the colonies. Here Schweitzer's health grew worse and pains developed.

One night the prisoners were ordered to pack quickly. The Schweitzers tried to make haste but though their belongings were few they were so slow at it that a guard threatened to make them leave the rest of their baggage behind. It was only at the last moment that he relented and even helped them pack.

They were taken to a great internment camp at Garaison in the Pyrenees mountains. On their arrival, an officer searched Schweitzer's belongings. He came upon a copy of a French translation of Aristotle's *Politics*. The officer was scandalized.

"How dare you bring political books into a camp of our enemy prisoners!"

Schweitzer gently explained that the book had been written many centuries ago and, therefore, could not do any harm.

"Well, we'll see if you're telling the truth," the officer said. He turned to an intelligent-looking fellow officer. "Look at this book and tell me if the Hun is telling the truth."

The officer looked and nodded.

The other grudgingly returned the book to Schweitzer. "Well, politics are a lot different from what they were then, so I see no harm in the book."

Schweitzer did not tell him that he was using the

book in connection with his criticism of the world of today.

Garaison, the Provençal word for healing, had formerly been a monastery to which many had made pilgrimages to be cured. Now it was a long-neglected collection of wind-swept cells, barely furnished and housing many more human beings than it had been designed to hold.

The Schweitzers had a small, bare cell to themselves.

The only comfort the place offered them was the rich variety of the human company there. They had been rounded up from all over the globe and from every walk of life. There were Germans and Austrians, scholars and shoemakers, bank directors and tailors, artists and hotelkeepers, engineers, waiters, cooks, and carpenters. There were Catholic priests and a group of other priests who wore white robes and red fezes. There were Arabs, Greeks, Chinese, Argentinians, East Indians, and Negroes from Liberia. There were Turks with their wives still wearing harem veils.

There was even a gypsy orchestra that had been playing in Paris and had been allowed to keep its instruments. A few days after their leader had been observing Schweitzer he came over to him and asked, "Are you by any chance the great organist Schweitzer of whom Romain Rolland has written in his book of the musicians of today?"

Schweitzer had met Romain Rolland, and the friendship that resulted remained long and fruitful. "Yes,"

Genius in the Jungle

Schweitzer told him, "M. Rolland did mention me in his book."

The gypsy beamed. "Then you must do us the honor of joining our orchestra as an honorary member. And are you or Madame Schweitzer about to have a birthday?"

Schweitzer thanked him for the honorary membership, and told him the date of his wife's birthday which was due in a few days.

The following Tuesday the Schweitzers were awakened by a serenade outside their cell, the full gypsy orchestra playing its wild, nostalgic music.

Another prisoner introduced himself to the Schweitzers. "My name is Borkeloh," he said, "I'm indebted to you for curing my wife at your hospital in Lambaréné. And I would like to do anything I can for you. Apart from liberty, what would you like to have most?"

"A table to write on," Schweitzer said, smiling, "because I could also play the organ on it."

He had answered jokingly and dismissed the matter from his mind.

But Borkeloh prowled about the vast, rambling monastery and had somehow managed to secure a few boards, tools, and nails, and one day came marching into Schweitzer's cell with a table.

"I wish you could hear the music that you have made possible for me," Schweitzer said to him.

Another former patient of Schweitzer's, a woman, recognized him and, seeing his wife suffering from the cold, made her accept some material that would make a warm dress if there were anyone there to sew it.

Word spread quickly at Garaison, and soon Mrs. Schweitzer was besieged by several men and women who had been skilled tailors and dressmakers, all begging for the chance to get the feel again of scissors, needle and thread, and material to work with.

Laughter was a rare but welcome visitor at Garaison, and a little of it came with a group of new prisoners who arrived and at once set up a complaint that the cooking was not good enough.

They complained so loudly that the Commandant summoned the group to his office. "May I ask you gentlemen what are your occupations?"

They told him. One had been a tailor, another a basket weaver, one had worked in a paint factory, a fourth had been a bricklayer.

"And you think you could do as well as my chefs, all of whom are professional?"

"We can do better," was the answer.

The Commandant stared, then said mildly, "Good. I will put you in charge of the kitchen. If you do not do better than my present chefs I will clap you behind bars as malcontents and troublemakers. However, you have the right to withdraw your complaint now and we will forget the whole matter."

The committee refused to withdraw the complaint and took up the Commandant's challenge.

To the amazement of the whole camp they made their boast good the very first day, with only potatoes

Genius in the Jungle

and cabbage as ingredients. It turned out that they had cooked at the war prison from which they had come, and in their eagerness to be kept busy they had become superb cooks.

Although Schweitzer was the only physician among the prisoners, he was strictly forbidden to do anything for the sick there, as there was an official camp doctor. But the camp doctor was an old country practitioner, and soon his work became too much for him to handle alone. Whereupon the Commandant let Schweitzer help, and gave him a cell to use as his office. "Thus I was a doctor once more," Schweitzer rejoiced.

But as usual he worried about his patients, and what saddened him most about them and multiplied his problems were the ills that came from lack of exercise—not of legs and arms, there was provision for that—but of talents and skills. He felt himself fortunate in this respect. He had lost his hospital, but he had his books to write and his organ on which to "practice." But these artists and artisans, executives and technicians, skilled and even unskilled workers were consumed by idleness, their abilities buried alive, without the mercy of oblivion, all craving to get at paints and canvas, piano, slide rule, lathe, trowel, plane, and what not. And since flesh and feeling are related as they are, frustration festered in them, and Schweitzer found many a case of asthma, ulcers, heart trouble, and other ailments which he knew how to cure but could not.

And often in spite of himself he had to intervene violently to restore peace among his fellow prisoners.

Many had lived long in France and were on the side of the Allies. Others remained violently German, and bloody clashes broke out that outraged Schweitzer.

But drained though he was of half his strength, his arms, huge and hairy, could still tear a fight apart, and in his anger that put theirs to shame for humanity and depth, he shook them sober.

He was acquiring, however, a rich and varied education. "One needed no books there to learn much. I made full use of my opportunities to learn from men with specialized knowledge of banking, architecture, factory building and equipment, cereal growing, furnace making and many other things that came to be of use to me later."

The winter was long and severe, and the cold in the Schweitzers' cell did not help their declining health.

In the spring the Schweitzers were transferred to another internment camp, this time at St. Rémy de Provence, where there were only Alsatians.

Here the Schweitzers caught up on news from home.

In Lambaréné, on what was perhaps his blackest day there, Schweitzer had already had tragic news about his mother. In a meaningless accident she had fallen in front of galloping cavalry and had been trampled to death.

The news the Schweitzers heard at St. Rémy was anything but reassuring. When at the outset of the war German troops poured into Alsace to defend it, officers warned their men that they were entering "hostile territory," so strong was the French sentiment there. Over

Genius in the Jungle

a thousand leading men and women in the province
were arrested as suspects or sympathizers with the
French. The use of the language was forbidden in the
streets, and thousands were deported to Germany for
other minor violations.

Now that Germany was losing the war, the inhabitants of Alsace had more reason to fear the future
than ever before. In their rage German troops had
threatened that if they had to leave Alsace there would
not be "one stone on another remaining."

At St. Rémy the tension of awaiting that outcome
was at least shared by fellow Alsatians. Schweitzer even
found old friends there. One was the son of "Daddy"
Iltis, and memories of his first organ teacher came back
to Schweitzer as he talked to the son, who was a
teacher, too. Another was formerly a pupil of Schweitzer's at the Theological Seminary and was now acting
as pastor at the internment camp. He would have gladly
stepped aside to let his old professor take his place, but
Schweitzer consented only to act as his assistant. It was,
however, a chance for him to renew his old and profound pleasure in preaching the Word.

And soon after his arrival Schweitzer was also made
camp doctor. Preaching and medical work would have
made a full day even for a man in good health. But
Schweitzer added "organ practice" on a table top, and
in addition somehow managed to put in some work on
his book on *The Decay of Civilization.*

Then one morning in July electrifying news came to
St. Rémy. Almost everyone there was listed to be freed

in an exchange of prisoners with the Germans, and the Alsatians were to be allowed to return to their homes by way of Switzerland.

22

SCHWEITZER had seen the list before his wife did. Her name was on it, but for some reason his was not. She assumed that it was, but he did not say anything about it until a few days later, when his name was added, too.

At sunrise one morning loaded lorries left St. Rémy and took their passengers to the railroad station at Tarascon. There they had to wait in a freight shed for their train to arrive at a station that was half a mile away.

The train whistle sounded and was the signal for hurry. Schweitzer shouldered as much of their baggage as he could. A cripple whom he had cured at the camp came up to him. "Please, may I help you?" he asked.

Genius in the Jungle

"I've nothing of my own to carry, so my hands are free."

Schweitzer was so touched that he thanked him and gave him a bundle that would be no burden but was big enough to make the cripple believe that he was helping importantly.

"While we walked along side by side, in the hot sun," Schweitzer wrote later, "I vowed that in thanks to him I would always keep a lookout for heavily laden people and help them. . . . On one occasion on the journey, however, when I tried it my offer was met with angry looks and suspicion. They thought I was trying to steal their baggage."

On its slow progress toward Switzerland more and more cars were added to the train.

Then the train crossed the border. For the first time in years Schweitzer saw smiling, peaceful country, untouched by war and prosperous in a setting of beauty that is better known perhaps than any other on earth.

When the train stopped at the station at Zurich the Schweitzers were astonished to hear their names called by people in the crowd on the platform. "Dr. Schweitzer!" "Albert!" "Helene!"

It was a group of university professors, musicians, and other friends of the past, who had known for some time that the Schweitzers would pass through the city and had come down to give them a heartfelt welcome.

"So we were not forgotten!" Schweitzer rejoiced.

It had been a minor grief with him that after nearly five years of war he was sure he and his wife had been forgotten in Europe, where everyone had had so many other and shattering concerns on their minds.

The greeting at Zurich, however, was only a fleeting pleasure to be forgotten when the train came to Constance on the German border. There the contrast between Switzerland and Germany was marked more vividly than on any child's most brightly colored map. On one side there was peace, on the other, war. The one was all the more beautiful now that the Schweitzers could see over the bristling barrier of bayonets and barbed wire into Germany.

For the first time Schweitzer saw what had once been beautiful stone buildings turned to rubble by bombardment from the air. He thought of all that had gone into putting up a single thatched-roof hut at Lambaréné. . . .

And as the train drew into the station at Constance the Schweitzers saw the faces that went with a losing war—pale, hungry, harassed.

Among them they caught sight of Helene's parents. . . .

The Bresslaus told them that as Günsbach was in the fighting zone Pastor Schweitzer had not been able to obtain permission to leave the village. The Germans in Alsace were being pressed back by the Allies but had stubbornly dug in, and the Münster valley was getting the brunt of artillery duels. Günsbach was the village nearest the front-line fighting. . . . No, the Bresslaus had not been there for a long time, and they had no news to give Schweitzer other than what he had already learned.

The Bresslaus had obtained permission to take their daughter back to their home in a distant suburb of Strasbourg, but Schweitzer would have to wait another day before he got his pass to go beyond Constance. Mrs. Schweitzer wanted to wait for him, but he would not listen. He insisted that she go at once to the first real comfort and shelter waiting for her after almost five years of hardship.

She needed it, and at once, and would for some months to come. For if nothing unfortunate happened in that arena where a war was raging to a furious climax, Mrs. Schweitzer would have a child sometime about the turn of the year.

So she went off with her parents.

Schweitzer reached Strasbourg the following evening. He had found night in the jungle an uneasy enough experience, but he had never before seen a European capital in a war blackout, where one had to grope blindly along great boulevards.

He was still groping in a dark and eerily silent city when suddenly the sirens sounded and rigid shafts of light shot aloft, feeling for the planes that were dropping their cargoes on the city.

It was out of the question for Schweitzer to get to the Bresslau home in the suburbs that night, and it was all he could do to find his way to Frau Fischer's rooming house near St. Thomas Church. There he stretched out on the first good bed he had had for ages, and he almost collapsed with exhaustion.

The next day he joined his wife at the Bresslaus.

Since Günsbach was in so active a war zone, it took Schweitzer many days of effort to obtain permission to go there. Even then he could not get a pass for his wife.

He was able to get to Colmar by train. After that there was no other transportation, and he had to set out for Günsbach on foot.

He forgot a violently protesting body in the anguish it cost him to see what had happened to the Münster valley. Village after village in ruins. The hills where he and other children "grew up like a bunch of wild roses" were now gashed and pocked with shellfire. The beechwood forest where as a boy Schweitzer and a stag had stared at each other for a wonderful moment was now hideous with splintered stumps and charred and broken limbs of trees.

And as though man had not done enough evil, there was a devastating drought, rare in that region, and dust clouds smoked everywhere.

In every village through which Schweitzer passed, there were notices posted up, instructing everyone to carry gas masks. Schweitzer had none.

As he limped along the last stretch toward Günsbach, he held his breath, straining for his first glimpse of it.

The church spire stood!

Günsbach stood!

Genius in the Jungle

As a boy Schweitzer used to think of the hills about the village as "sheltering it." He never dreamed how literally true it would turn out. Günsbach was huddled so low among those hills that artillery fire passed harmlessly over it.

But the village streets seethed with German uniforms and the come-and-go of motorcycles, military trucks, and light artillery.

Outside the parsonage Schweitzer's father hurried to meet him, looking older in face and figure but radiant at the sight of his son.

23

THE parsonage itself was crowded with German officers quartered there and the many who came and went on military errands. Pastor Schweitzer told his son that he had forgotten how it felt to be free of them.

But the pastor had kept his son's old room ready for his return.

Schweitzer went up and lay down on the bed there to rest, and what he now heard in the hills was no soft summer thunder. The fighting was so close that the villagers had been ordered to hold themselves in readiness to evacuate at a moment's notice.

The pastor showed his son the cellar shelter against air raids where he must go the moment the warning siren sounded. But he himself had become so used to the siren that he ignored it and went on working in his study.

The drought had killed all the food and fodder crops, and in his room Schweitzer now heard the lowing of hungry cattle.

Thunderheads piled up in the sky, but they brought only winds that dried what little moisture remained in the soil, and instead of rain great clouds of dust settled on all the countryside.

Schweitzer finally obtained the necessary pass, and brought his wife to Günsbach. She had hoped that the air of his home hills, that had saved him when he was an infant, would help to restore his health now. But her heart sank when she saw him.

He was so elated, however, at having her with him that he found the courage to do something he had been postponing. He climbed up to the organ loft and sat down at the first console he had touched since he had left Europe. His heart must have misbehaved as he waited to see how much of his touch on the organ was still with him.

He did not find out that day, for he had to go back

to bed at once. For the past few weeks he had been running high temperatures, and pain was getting worse.

There is a revealing snapshot that had been taken at Lambaréné. A Pahouin youth, incurably ill and in pain, saw a visitor with a camera, became curious, and was shown what it would do. He begged to be photographed together with Schweitzer. In the snapshot the two sit side by side, the youth's face contorted with pain. Schweitzer was never the man to parade his emotions, and in the photograph he was trying to look composed, but the lines on his face clearly parallel those of the youth, and it is just as clear that Schweitzer was utterly unconscious of it. Long before that he had formulated his feeling that pain establishes a brotherhood among those who have lived with it. If anyone did not need to have that lesson taught him, it was Schweitzer. But life, with its own logic, or an insane lack of it, was grinding it into him now.

Nor was his own pain all that he was going through. All the world was in the throes, and Schweitzer, as much involved in it as in his personal life, and on occasion more so, had to endure, in addition to everything else, the thought of how little use he was to it now.

He would have been less than human, therefore, if he did not indulge in at least a groan of frustration. "I felt much like a coin that has rolled under a piece of furniture and has remained there, lost."

His fever and pain grew steadily worse until by the end of August it was clear he was due for a major operation without delay.

Albert Schweitzer

There was no way for him to get to Colmar, where he could take the train for Strasbourg, except by walking. His wife insisted upon going along, and all his stern efforts to dissuade her were in vain.

One morning soon after, the two set out on foot. Somehow they managed to get halfway to Colmar, when a wagon came along and gave them a lift.

On September first an eminent surgeon, Professor Stultz, operated on Schweitzer. When the patient came out of the ether he asked for a report on himself. Professor Stultz did not sound reassuring. There might have to be at least another operation.

Life was no longer lavish with Schweitzer as he lay on the hospital bed. The doctor was sick. The philanthropist was not only poor but deep in debt. The man to whom so many had turned for help now did not know how he would support even his small family.

24

BUT as soon as Schweitzer could walk about he was offered medical charge of two small wards at a Strasbourg hospital. The pay would be small, the work hard, "but I joyfully accepted the post."

At the same time life seemed to have come the full round for him in regard to the Church of St. Nicholas. During his medical course, when he had had to give up preaching, he had avoided passing the church to keep from thinking about it. Now he was offered a post as assistant there, and this, too, he "joyfully accepted."

Although the fighting in Alsace, as elsewhere, was mounting in fury, it was going against the Germans, and the pro-German head of the Church of St. Nicholas decided that it was a good time for him to resign. This made Schweitzer acting head, and with the position went the use of the parish house, a welcome help to a man expecting an increase in his family.

"During the little free time which my two posts left me I occupied myself with . . ."

First he tried working on a book about Bach's Choral Preludes, but the manuscript he had begun at Lambaréné was still there, and though he had sent for it he had reason to believe it would not arrive for a long time, if ever.

Then he resumed work on his Philosophy of Civilization, but those manuscripts were also at Lambaréné, and he could not wait for them to arrive.

Whereupon he launched on an examination of the great world religions, studying them in the light of his own philosophy of reverence for life.

At this time the German military chiefs, Generals Hindenburg and Ludendorf, their backs against the wall, decided to gamble their men on a final effort, win all or lose all. Throwing everything they had into it, they lashed out in an offensive that won more ground every day than they had ever gained before, until a horrified world believed everything lost. But the Commander of the Allied Armies, General Foch, was also gambling, but more wisely. He let the Germans outrun their strength, deliberately giving ground before them, until the right moment. Then he struck, and the Germans crumbled, this time for good.

On November 11, 1918, jubilee bells rang out all over the world.

Alsace was free and French again, and never before did the bells of the Strasbourg Cathedral send such a surge of emotion through Schweitzer's heart. . . .

And on his birthday, on January 14th, his daughter was born.

Genius in the Jungle

The second major operation came off successfully, in the summer of that year.

With it hope came seeping back into the man, but not full confidence, it seems. For when he received a letter from Barcelona inviting him to play the organ again for his old friends at the Orféo Català, he was almost afraid to accept.

To play the organ again after so many years away from it . . . before musicians who had heard him at his best. . . .

There would be no pay for the recital, not even traveling expenses. But Schweitzer "scraped together every shilling" he could, obtained permission to travel —there was only armistice as yet, not peace with its freedom of movement—and set off for Barcelona.

Whatever his emotions were throughout the return trip, he came back to Strasbourg considerably heartened. His playing had been warmly applauded, although he could not tell how much of that warmth was due to his being a guest playing for profoundly gracious hosts. But he had a tremulous feeling that perhaps he was still "an artist of some value."

He went back to his hospital duties and to his work at the Church of St. Nicholas, to his book on world religion, to his organ practice, this time on magnificent instruments . . . and he was now also a father. And since the day was not long enough for all this, he went back to his old neglect of sleep, and almost managed it, though not quite.

He was still not his old self.

Albert Schweitzer

It was a busy life, and, though humble in scope compared to the old days when the capitals of Europe heard him play and the great universities invited him to lecture before them, something of the old glow crept back into his blood.

Nevertheless it *was* all on a humble plane, not like the rich days on which he had turned his back on his thirtieth birthday. The great universities seemed to have forgotten him.

But in Sweden its leading churchman, Archbishop Söderblom, whose works on religious philosophy had influenced Schweitzer, had been wondering what had become of the promising young scholar who had so impressed him years before with his analyses of Jesus, St. Paul, and Kant. He made inquiries.

One morning shortly before that Christmas Schweitzer found an impressive-looking envelope with the University of Upsala crest upon it.

The Schweitzers opened it together. It was an invitation from Archbishop Söderblom to deliver a series of lectures for the Olaus-Petri Foundation at the University of Upsala, which is one of the oldest seats of learning in the world. The subjects of the lectures were left to Schweitzer, and the university asked "the privilege of publishing the lectures."

Archbishop Söderblom . . . the University of Upsala . . . the subjects of the lectures to be anything Schweitzer chose . . . "the privilege of publishing" them requested . . . Schweitzer found the invitation almost too much for him, after so long an absence from scholarly audiences and so soon after an operation from which he had not fully recovered.

He wrote the Archbishop feelingly, thanking him for the honor of the invitation but doubting whether his physical condition justified the risks of accepting it. His wife, too, he wrote, had not recovered her health, and he could not very well leave her.

Archbishop Söderblom cheerfully reassured him. There were excellent physicians in Sweden, he wrote, and he would see to it that the Schweitzers got the best medical care. The climate of Sweden would brace them, and the Archbishop's wife, who kept an excellent table, promised to fatten them up.

Schweitzer wrote back, accepting for himself and his wife.

25

LEAVING their child with the Bresslaus, the Schweitzers arrived in Sweden still "tired, depressed, and ailing." They were taken into the warmhearted family life of the Söderbloms and fed, catered to, and spoiled as they never had been in their lives.

Nevertheless it was an inwardly nervous man who faced his audience at the first of the Olaus-Petri lectures. Schweitzer had chosen his philosophy of civilization as his subject, and since the material he needed for reference had not yet arrived from Lambaréné, he had had to rewrite it from memory.

Applause broke out throughout the lecture which could not be mistaken for mere courtesy. He could see the faces of his audiences as he spoke, and the discussions that followed were like fresh mountain air to the man from the tropics.

He had not lost ground. . . .

His last lecture was on his own thesis, reverence for life. He had hardly begun speaking when he felt such an electric atmosphere of response and was so deeply moved by it that he found it difficult to speak.

Genius in the Jungle

In the weeks that followed, the health of the Schweitzers improved, their spirits rose, and they had gained prestige, and a new host of friends.

Nevertheless, one day when Schweitzer and the Archbishop were out walking, sharing an umbrella in the light spring shower, the Archbishop noticed a shadow on Schweitzer's spirits. He asked if Schweitzer would care to tell him what was troubling him.

After some hesitation Schweitzer told him. During the war, when costs had gone up enormously at Lambaréné and Schweitzer's funds had run out, he had borrowed heavily from friends who could not well afford to lose the money they had so readily lent him. He told the Archbishop how much.

Söderblom nodded; it was quite a sum.

But why not give lectures, he asked Schweitzer, and recitals, charging admission?

Schweitzer pointed out that while a university audience understood his German and French, a wider public might not.

The Archbishop said he would get him a translator.

As to concerts, Schweitzer went on, he had given only one in all these years since he had abandoned the organ for Africa, and while the one audience had responded warmly, they were, after all, his hosts, and he could not expect the same tolerance from the general public who paid to hear professional performances.

Try it, Söderblom suggested.

He arranged a concert, and Schweitzer sat down at the organ to play to a packed house. In his book on

Bach he had written that to play the composer properly one must possess profound serenity, and Schweitzer did not feel profoundly serene.

Yet the program was all Bach.

When the last note of the first number had died away and Schweitzer's hands dropped, moist with apprehension, there was applause, of course. He had expected a certain amount of courteous acknowledgment But the applause was continuing . . . and he could no longer mistake its meaning.

He must have recovered concert pitch!

The critics said so in print next morning. Their reviews heartened him, and the concerts that followed drew even better notices.

Financially, too, they were heartening.

Then there were the lectures. At Lambaréné on occasional Sundays Schweitzer would give short sermons that were translated sentence by sentence into Galoa and Pahouin. Now a young Swedish theological student did the same for Schweitzer at his lectures. There he also told his audiences about Lambaréné.

He was talking of something that meant much to him, and though it was in a foreign tongue the translator lost nothing of the vividness of the theme—the struggle in the jungle between the manifold onslaughts there on the human flesh and spirit, and the attempt to counteract them. The pictures he presented were fascinating enough. But the audience saw something the speaker was not aware of, a dedicated man, glowing with spirit and not at all conscious that he was anything more than the narrator.

And the man and his message moved them to give him more than applause. They knew that the Jungle Hospital, as he called it, was in debt, and they took it as a privilege to help him.

He in turn gave to the Swedes something they would have discarded as useless until he made them see its value—their old church organs.

"Though they are not large," he wrote, "the wonderfully resonant old Swedish organs pleased me greatly. They were admirably adapted to my method of playing Bach."

As a result of his tour two organizations were formed, The Friends of Lambaréné, and an association for the safeguarding of old organs.

The Friends of Lambaréné became the parent body of other such groups elsewhere and helped relieve Schweitzer of the money worries that had so plagued him.

He now had enough to pay off his hospital's debts. Meanwhile Archbishop Söderblom told a publisher that there was a good story in Schweitzer's African experiences. The result was a book by Schweitzer, *On the Edge of the Primeval Forest*, which was translated into Swedish, English, Dutch, French, Danish, and Finnish. It not only brought him royalties but made Lambaréné known to an ever-increasing public throughout Europe and America.

And with something of a return of life's former

generosity to him there came an offer from Switzerland that would not only solve his personal economic problems but would give direction to his life thereafter. The Theological Faculty of the University of Zurich gave him an honorary degree of Doctor of Divinity; and if he wanted to teach in Switzerland there was the offer of a career.

It seemed like a good dream come true. Switzerland, the land of peace, at the very heart of Europe and yet untouched by its decay and its many wars—what an ideal setting in which to study the sick continent and to seek its cure. . . .

Even personal considerations made the offer attractive. His wife was still ailing, and mountain air was what she needed. And their child would grow up in surroundings whose outward beauty matched a history that was good to contemplate by comparison even with his own beloved but war-torn Alsace. . . .

He consulted his wife, and she was radiant at the prospect of their living there.

He sent word to Switzerland that they might expect him.

The Schweitzers left Sweden with their health improved, and with that blend of regret and promises of reunion that go with the good-bys to a happy visit.

It was only when Schweitzer was alone that something of shadow came back to him.

For he had been hearing from Lambaréné. At first the letters had been few, cautiously impersonal, letters from Frenchmen to a German subject, though at Lambaréné they never thought of him that way. But military censors would be reading the letters—inquiries about his wife's health and his, and bits of news of the little world at Lambaréné.

Now that Alsace was French again and Schweitzer was a French citizen, the letters came more often and were fullhearted. There was also a note of urgency in them, a call repeated and growing. Doctor, they miss you . . . Doctor, they need you . . . Doctor, you must come back. . . . For mercy's sake, Doctor . . .

He heard voices in those letters, the ones whose agony he had stilled with his first surgical operation at Lambaréné, and on his last day there. . . . There were others, too. . . . He would have to be deaf indeed not to hear them now.

But he was needed in Europe as well. His wife had not yet recovered from Africa, and now there was their small daughter to whom he owed something as well.

Also, he had been a teacher before he had turned doctor, and they were asking him to come back and teach. Is not teaching also an imperative service, in a world that knows no better than to turn to war for a solution? He had something he wanted desperately to offer as an alternative. He needed time and an untroubled mind to develop his message, "Revere life!"

And not all who turn to music do so in the mood for luxury. Music can be an act of worship, and not all worship is adoration and ecstasy. There is a simple hymn that Bach had set to music, one of his Chorales, "I Call Upon Thee, Jesus," that is as poignant a plea for help as any that comes from a sufferer with strangulated hernia. The only difference is that a scream of pain is only a cry, and is not in itself relief. Whereas a call of the other kind is somehow, subtly, already a help, most of all when it has been translated by such a master as Bach. . . . But Bach has left only marks on paper and others must interpret him.

There were increasing calls for Schweitzer to play him, and was this not a service, too?

But Schweitzer would have been the first to acknowledge that now there were others who were performing that service through every known medium of music, artists far greater than he.

Whereas along the Ogowé there was still not a single doctor for many hundred miles around.

26

SCHWEITZER talked things over with his wife, and she agreed that he was needed in Lambaréné and must go back.

The only question was, could she go along. There was no question, of course, of taking Rhena, their daughter, to Africa.

What could be postponed was the decision as to whether Mrs. Schweitzer could go with her husband. Her last stay in Africa was still with her and would take some time to shake off.

The decision could be postponed because Schweitzer meant to stay on in Europe until he had established a solid financial base for the hospital at Lambaréné, not only to rebuild it but to expand. In addition, he must earn enough to provide for his family for the years he would be away.

The Schweitzers went back to Strasbourg and resumed family life in the parsonage of the Church of St. Nicholas.

But the increasing work on his books, the heavy cor-

respondence from the many who had become interested
in the Jungle Hospital, and the recitals and lecture tours
that were being organized for him made it necessary
for him to give up his two Strasbourg posts, the hospital and the Church of St. Nicholas.

He moved his family to his father's roomy parsonage
at Günsbach. Its sky and earth would always mean
home to him more than any other place on earth; and
he wanted it to mean that for his wife and Rhena.

Some of the scars on the countryside were healing.
The drought, too, had passed, and several seasons of
favorable weather had brought back much of the Münster valley's former bloom.

For a brief spell before he settled down to his busy
life Schweitzer indulged himself in Günsbach. He
needed the rest that came with the renewal of his ties
there, memories of the past and the resumption of old
and new contacts with his neighbors.

Some of his old schoolmates and neighbors were
dead, and when he learned of it he wrote: "One thing
that moves me as I look back on my young days is the
fact that so many people had given me something of
value without their knowing it. The realization of it
comes home sometimes only as we look back, just as the
full beauty of a certain piece of music or of a land-
scape comes to us only in recollection. . . . Many a
time now, with a feeling of shame, have I said quietly
over a grave the words I should have uttered when they
could have been heard."

He seemed to find it natural on occasion to help his

father in the pulpit or in the organ loft. The least-informed of the villagers now knew that the world outside was turning with respect to the parson's son; that when he was in the pulpit of their church they were listening to the man who had once been head of the Theological School of the University; and that when he played for them they were hearing one of the great organists of the age.

Yet, when they talked to him face to face, they grew a little confused. How can one be so important in the world and not know it?

But calls from the world outside increasingly took him away from Günsbach.

The first time that Spain ever heard Bach's St. Matthew's Passion was when Schweitzer accompanied it on the organ in Barcelona.

Switzerland called him to play the organ and to give lectures. Then Sweden again. In England he gave the Dale Memorial Lectures at Cambridge, others at Birmingham. Then there were more tours in Sweden and in England again; another in Denmark.

In Czechoslovakia he lectured under the auspices of Professor Oscar Kraus, and out of it came a new experience for Schweitzer. Professor Kraus published a life of Schweitzer, with an interpretation of his philosophy.

In the spring of 1923 Schweitzer finished the first of his two volumes on the *Philosophy of Civilization.*

In the same summer he produced a little book in what must be a speed record hard to beat. He was passing through Zurich and between trains stopped off to visit a friend, Dr. Oscar Pfister, a psychoanalyst. Schweitzer wanted to stretch out and rest, and Dr. Pfister wanted some material for an analysis of a remarkable man. He told Schweitzer to relax on the couch, but while he did so, to tell as much as he could of his childhood and youth.

Dr. Pfister took down in shorthand everything Schweitzer said. A few hours later Schweitzer caught his train. But his spontaneous recital of his early days came out as a book, Schweitzer's *Memoirs of Childhood and Youth.*

One gets glimpses of Schweitzer at this time through the eyes of others—journalists, for instance, like Hubert Peet, who accompanied him on one of his English tours. "It was a strenuous time," he wrote, "conveying the burly black-cloaked figure from one theologian to another, from one organ recital to another."

Schweitzer played the organ in historic Westminster Abbey, and Peet describes him at rehearsal there, in "the faint glimmer of the dying day that showed in subdued colors the ancient stained glass of its windows, and touched here and there the gold carvings of the altar screen."

A Danish organist followed him from one concert to another to learn the secret of the man's distinctive touch on the instrument.

Then for weeks Schweitzer turned pupil again, taking courses in obstetrics and in dentistry, in preparation for Lambaréné.

He designed a small hospital ward of corrugated iron

that was made in sections, packed, and shipped off to Africa.

Then came the shopping for the thousand and one items that would be needed for an expanded hospital in Lambaréné.

He was ready to leave for Africa now, for with all his activities he had accumulated enough money for his twofold needs: his family and Lambaréné.

But Europe was running a mounting fever, especially Germany, and much as Schweitzer's mind was on Africa he had to give heed to what was going on about him.

In a strange incident he was even affected personally. The presses were rolling in Nördlingen, Bavaria, turning out Schweitzer's book on the decay of civilization and how to arrest it, when a sinister chain of events stopped the printing.

The immediate reason for it was that there was no more paper available for books. The government needed all the blank paper it could get for use in printing money, and it could not get enough. It was not that the government was so rich. On the contrary, it was so poor that its money was becoming worthless, and more and more of it had to be printed. Before the war a German mark was worth almost an American quarter. At the time the press was stopped for lack of paper for Schweitzer's books, a street beggar would have refused a hundred million marks, for they would not have bought him so much as a match, and every day the purchasing power of the mark diminished by half.

Albert Schweitzer

The plight of the German people was so desperate that millions of them were listening to a man who had been a failure in every effort of his life up to then, except in his talent for hatred. Adolf Hitler had a simple message for them.

"Follow me, throw the government out, let us arm, and I promise you that in a few years we will have the world at our feet!"

That autumn he and a handful of followers did try to seize power in Bavaria. As they marched up a main thoroughfare of Munich they thought that the population would arise and join them. Instead, police met them and fired. Some of Hitler's comrades fell. Hitler flung himself down in the mud, then escaped.

The "Beer Hall Revolution," as Hitler's attempt was called, looked farcical to many. But in the minds of the more thoughtful it looked like a rehearsal, with more serious performances to come.

Schweitzer knew it, and he knew that eventually it would affect everything that was vital to him, and that meant all of humanity. But, sick as humanity was, he could only prescribe for it, as he did in his books. But in Lambaréné they needed his eyes and hands, his surgery. . . .

A young medical student, Noel Gillespie, was going to Africa with him to help him at Lambaréné for a time.

Mrs. Schweitzer could not go. Her health was still not equal to it, and there was Rhena to consider.

That meant a separation from her husband for a year or two, perhaps longer, but she agreed to it.

"Unceasingly I thank her in my heart," Schweitzer wrote in tribute to her decision and to her lifelong help to him.

He and Gillespie boarded the Dutch freighter *Orestes* on February 21, 1924, at Bordeaux, bound for Africa.

27

THE voyage to Africa was uneventful except to a woman whose baby Schweitzer and Gillespie helped usher into the world. Schweitzer's version of it was that the mother "took advantage" of the presence of a doctor on board who was fresh from a course in obstetrics. Gillespie received an intensive, if uncomfortable, course in infant feeding, as he had to prepare the newcomer's bottle eight times a day, twenty-four hours round.

At Cape Lopez, Schweitzer and Gillespie transferred

to the steamer *Alembe*, which had become ramshackle and dirty since Schweitzer had seen it last. But the warmth of welcome he received from the officers and crew and some of the passengers who had known him more than made up for what the vessel had lost in looks.

There was considerable talk on the boat of the recent activities of "leopard men," with their latest victim a native of Lambaréné. Schweitzer had known of these men even before he had come to the Gabon for the first time. But young Gillespie stared almost with disbelief as he listened.

The "leopard men" were a secret society of savages who went about armed either with real leopard claws or steel imitations. Their victims looked as though they had been killed by real leopards, with claw marks on the throat, and there were even leopard tracks on the jungle floor.

Motives for murder by "leopard men" ranged from revenge to killing for hire. What disquieted Schweitzer most was the darkness of mind that enabled them to get ever new recruits. Their method was to induce some unsuspecting native to drink with them, then they told him that he had just partaken of human blood brewed in a skull and that the magic in it left him no choice except to join their band. Otherwise he was doomed to die of indescribable tortures by the evil spirits he had antagonized.

Caught between two terrors, of the men confronting him and of the evil powers he could not see, a native almost invariably chose what would pacify both, and he joined the "leopard men."

His first assignment was to lure a relative into the jungle where the band could get him as its victim. This was only a test. If the candidate met it, he became a member of the band. If he failed, he was killed.

The plague of "leopard men" was spreading so widely over Africa that even Scotland Yard was called in to stamp it out. While the whites were not in danger, they felt for the terrified native population, and while Scotland Yard and the Colonial police hunted the "leopard men," schools and missions did their utmost to try to make the natives see that there were no spirits as evil as the "leopard men" themselves.

Schweitzer now determined to join the crusade of education and to make Sunday services at the hospital a more important activity than ever before.

Just then, however, Schweitzer's greatest anxiety was the fate of the hospital he had left behind.

When his canoe came within sight of the mission he strained for his first glimpse of the hospital buildings. The familiar skyline was overgrown with jungle.

The first moment that the lavish welcome prepared by the mission was over, Schweitzer hurried up the hill.

He had expected to see deterioration, but not the ruin that confronted him. The lane between the buildings was now a young jungle. Even the walls of corrugated iron were almost rotted through with rust. Practically nothing was left of the raffia-tiled roofs, and the rainy season was on. It meant that deadly sun would be pouring in by day, and torrents at night.

It was the day before Easter Sunday and the missionaries had expected that the doctor and Gillespie would spend the holiday in ease.

But an hour after their arrival Schweitzer and Gillespie were off in a canoe on a hunt for roof tiles.

They already knew that it would be hard hunting. The tiles were of raffia woven over bamboo, took skill and considerable time to make, and the natives were busy at better-paying labor in the lumber camps.

Schweitzer and Gillespie got out at a village an hour from Lambaréné and received a royal greeting. Schweitzer responded with warmth that was remarkable even for him, but he had an ulterior motive.

"I should like to forget," he wrote later, "the amount of flattery I had to hand out in order to coax some grass tiles from my friends."

He needed five hundred tiles.

He got sixty-four.

He threatened that he would not treat a single patient from that village unless they gave him more. They laughed in his face. Coming from "our Doctor," such a threat sounded more like a joke, which it was more or less.

The two men got back to the mission in darkness and in a downpour, and Schweitzer tried to find comfort in the fact that at least sixty-four holes in his roofs would be covered.

They had dinner at the mission, then they went to

Schweitzer's house for their first night. It had become so weakened that a heavy storm had almost wrecked it, and it had been saved only by hard work and oak planks.

As it was, Schweitzer found only two of the four rooms available for them that night. A third was occupied temporarily by one of the missionaries, while the fourth resounded with the angry buzzing of a swarm of wild bees that had long set up housekeeping in it.

part four

———

28

WORD got out into the jungle quickly that the doctor was back, and the patients came flocking in on Monday. The reopened hospital got off to a depressing start. Schweitzer sat up all one night trying to save a desperate heart case but lost him by morning. As he left the dead man, Schweitzer had the novel experience of seeing a native child, a little girl, run away shrieking at the sight of him.

She ran into the mission school crying that Schweitzer was a "leopard man " An amazed teacher demanded an explanation.

"I saw him take a man into the hospital alive," the

little girl sobbed, "now he's dead. I tell you, the doctor killed him! Why do they let a white leopard man go free and put the black ones in prison?"

The sixty-four tiles did little to protect the patients that Schweitzer had to keep on at the hospital. A drenching in that climate is, for a variety of reasons, a more serious matter than elsewhere and two of Schweitzer's patients died because he had not enough roof tiles.

Roof tiles become an obsession with Schweitzer.

When he delivered a newborn in one of the villages he demanded tiles in payment. "My moral sense was going."

A village chief was brought to the hospital with an injured hand. At once he became impatient because he was not getting the attention that he felt was due his exalted station.

Schweitzer explained that many others were sick there too and required attention.

That did not matter, said the chief; the others were not chiefs.

It did matter, Schweitzer pointed out mildly; the hospital was for all, but he would see what he could do for him in the way of special attention. Meanwhile would His Majesty look at those roofs and see how badly many tiles were needed. It would help matters very much if he could contribute some.

"I'll see about it when I get back to my village."

That might take considerable time, Schweitzer said, looking pensively at the chief's injury. Meanwhile it would help many suffering men and women if the chief could see his way to sending word to his village that three hundred tiles were to be brought quickly. It would even help cure the chief's hand.

The chief was outraged. Not a tile more than one hundred, was his offer.

They settled on a promise of two hundred tiles.

Schweitzer treated the injury with a great show of concern, but a week passed and no tiles came. The chief's excuses were so transparent that finally Schweitzer said he would not look at the chief's hand until the tiles came.

By then the chief had come to know Schweitzer well. He grinned. The threat did not seem to work.

Schweitzer had always thought of himself as possessed of a terrible temper. It was true that whenever his sense of right and human kindness was outraged his indignation was profound. At such times his great body and majestic anger were something to see. The chief saw it now, as Schweitzer walked away without a word.

What the chief did not know was that Schweitzer was putting on an act. When no one came near the chief for days he became panicky. He also did not know that his hand was getting well of its own accord.

He found Schweitzer and promised fervently that he would send for the two hundred tiles, only the doctor must look at his hand at once.

Schweitzer coldly announced that the price had risen to five hundred tiles.

"Five hundred, then, only cure my hand!"

Schweitzer examined it gravely and put some needless medication on it. The chief at once felt practically cured, went back to his village, and Schweitzer did not get a single tile.

"Nevertheless in his own way," Schweitzer wrote later, "he is quite a fine fellow."

Meanwhile the holes in the roofs affected not only the patients but also the doctor. Working inside was so unendurably hot that Schweitzer neglected wearing his sun helmet, and suffered "several slight sunstrokes." The exhaustion they brought on was not slight.

But he sent out word so emphatically that patients who expected treatment at the hospital would have to pay with grass tiles that tiles began coming in. By Whitsunday he had enough for his roofs, though not the reserves he needed.

It took experts, however, to mend the roofs, and Schweitzer's problem now was to get enough labor, for that and for a multitude of other jobs about the hospital which had to be done.

But even before the tiles had helped, he had already devised a way of protecting some of the sick from exposure, now that the rains were coming. He had beds built in double tiers where the roofs did afford protection.

Schweitzer had made it a principle that every patient should pay something, no matter how little, for the service, which would help the hospital as well as the patient's self-respect. It remained more principle than practice. It would have been impossible for Schweitzer to turn away a sufferer who was too poor to pay, or even one who re-fused payment.

But he did succeed in getting a certain amount of labor out of such patients as could help and from their friends and families who were staying on, waiting to take them back cured.

Schweitzer had to be foreman as well as doctor, other-wise no work would be done. Early every morning he had to recruit his work gang, some days having as many as fifteen. On other mornings he would find that every one of his crew had gone fishing or back to his village for a visit.

When he did get a number of them to work he had to stand watch over them all the time. As a foreman, he sometimes had to resort to unique methods to keep the crew at work. One day, for instance, several of his men were on a roof at work on the gaps in it. Lunchtime came, and his workers made for the ladder. Schweitzer saw storm clouds coming fast and asked the men to keep on working until they had finished that particular job. There would be just enough time before the storm broke.

But the workmen insisted on their rights to lunch and a rest, though in reality they were not as badly in need of it as patients were in need of protection against the coming rain.

Schweitzer won the argument by the simple expedi-ent of taking the ladder away before they could come down.

But at Lambaréné the moment one problem was

Albert Schweitzer

solved, and even before that, others came clamoring for solution.

Food for the patients had always been a problem for Schweitzer, more or less, and now it became more so. Invariably patients and those who had brought them consumed more than they had brought along. Schweitzer had to furnish the difference.

In ordinary times Schweitzer could cope with the situation. He had bought large stocks of rice, dried fish, manioc—the starch staple of the region—and for fats there were either palm oil or canned vegetable fat imported from Europe.

The patients cooked the food themselves.

At midday came the line-up for the day's food ration.

Schweitzer had to stand over the distribution, to see to it that only those who were entitled received any. But almost everyone who came made a decision necessary, there were so many impostors.

They had a wealth of claims, some real, others less so. Sometimes he had to use the wisdom of Solomon. A patient would tell him that his village had stopped sending him food for this or that plausible reason. Schweitzer knew that it was partly true, but the real reason was that the village knew Schweitzer would not let the patient starve. What was he to do? Of course he fed him.

But he gave each case rigid scrutiny, and with time he had to assume that most applicants for food were lying about their claims until they proved otherwise.

Then one day even that attitude broke down. A patient and his wife had not asked for their rations, and

Schweitzer, seeing them look hungry, asked them why they did not come to the midday distribution.

With quiet dignity they told him. They had seen the skepticism with which Schweitzer had met most of the stories and rather than have him suspect them of lying they had gone without food.

Whereupon Schweitzer turned the job of food distribution over to a dependable native.

Occasionally items of food that would be unique in a European hospital helped out the food supply. One of the men at the mission saw a boa constrictor near the girl's school and, running into Schweitzer's house, took his gun and shot it. Schweitzer's account of it was: "As it was shot with my gun, I got, as was fitting, half of it for the hospital. Unfortunately it was only five-and-a-half feet long and not very fat. The patients very nearly came to blows over the distribution of this dainty."

All this time Noel Gillespie was as busy as Schweitzer. Like Schweitzer, too, Gillespie had to perform many functions besides those at the clinic.

A patient, N'Gonde, a woodcutter by trade, had come to the hospital stricken with sleeping sickness, which the natives with good reason called "the killing sickness." Suddenly he went into a phase of it dangerous to others, violent insanity. While Schweitzer kept him quiet with sedatives, Gillespie, a good carpenter, built a cell of planks, and N'Gonde was locked in it.

Gillespie had scarcely finished N'Gonde's cell than the chicken house fell in. Termites had been at it. Gillespie was at work repairing it when the floor gave under him. Now repairs were out of the question because all the wood was so rotten that no nail would hold any two pieces together, so a new hen house had to be built, and in a hurry. The old one was no longer any protection against the snakes and the leopards that were common hazards there.

While Gillespie was busy with the hen house N'Gonde broke out of his cell. As fast as Gillespie could fix one weak spot in it N'Gonde found new ones.

Matters were not made easier for Schweitzer and Gillespie by the increasing practice on the part of the native villagers of dumping their dying on the hospital grounds during the night. Because of the witch doctors' rejection of all patients they did not think they could cure, it threw a staggering problem and burden on Schweitzer's shoulders.

He could not very well send them away, and he did not, yet it not only meant a great increase in the death rate of the hospital, with a corresponding depression of Schweitzer's spirits, but also, since he had no separate ward for hopeless cases, their dying also depressed the other patients.

This meant additional pressure on him to build greater facilities, and he had to do as much of the building as any of the workers under him. "The double burden of builder and doctor," as Schweitzer put it, in turn laid still another burden upon him, perhaps one of the hardest that a conscientious physician is called upon to bear.

"How I suffered because I could not make my examinations of patients as thorough as they should have been . . . and because I could not give sufficient time for each patient. . . . How often the microscope and the test tube should have been used, and were not!"

Worst of all to bear were the calls for surgery that he could not meet because he had only two hands and there are only twenty-four hours in a day.

29

BUT almost always when he seemed at the end of his resources there would come a measure of relief to Schweitzer, most of it due, however, to his own efforts.

The cure for some of the common and usually fatal diseases of the region was some specific drug, and Schweitzer had many occasions on which to use it. A recurrent note in his letters, however, was, "Unfortunately this drug is very expensive."

Now he was running short of even inexpensive drugs. But just as he was wondering when, if ever, a big shipment of drugs that he had ordered would arrive, it came.

And just as Noel Gillespie, now due back at his studies in England, was leaving, there arrived a tall, smiling young woman, Mathilde Kottman, a volunteer nurse. She had heard much of Schweitzer's work and had written, offering to help. He had accepted but also warned her of the many hardships she must expect. Now she was at Lambaréné, radiating more confidence than Schweitzer felt at any newcomer's ability to last there.

But within a week kerosene lamps at the hospital were properly tended, there was always enough boiled water at the surgery, clean laundry accumulated, the chickens were better cared for, more eggs found their way to the sick instead of "taking a walk," the fate of almost any article that was not closely watched. The value of the article did not matter. Someone even stole a book of Bach's organ pieces which Schweitzer had laboriously annotated for playing.

But Schweitzer rejoiced. "Never again will some of us find our beds made with tablecloths instead of sheets. . . . The clouds are beginning to lift."

Then Joseph Azvawami came back. Schweitzer had been sure that he had lost him to the lumber business. But Joseph had felt the call to resume his post as "First Assistant to the Doctor of Lambaréné," as he had styled himself. Leaving his wife to take care of the business, he announced that he would stay on at the hospital unless some emergency called him back to business.

Noel Gillespie left for Europe, amid heartfelt farewells from natives and whites.

But shortly after that Schweitzer went down to the landing to welcome a new arrival, Doctor Victor Nessman, the son of an Alsatian pastor who had been a fellow student of Schweitzer's at the University of Strasbourg.

Schweitzer's heart beat hard. A *doctor* to help him! He must have breathed a prayer for the newcomer to be especially competent as well as willing, as he would have to be at Lambaréné.

A stripling, almost a boy in looks, waved to Schweitzer from the canoe as it neared the landing. The young man called out, "You're going to rest now, Doctor, for I'm taking over all the work."

He said it with the cockiness of one who has just been given a diploma certifying his right to deal with life and death.

Schweitzer could forgive it, but he decided that a little lesson in life at Lambaréné would not do the young doctor harm. He looked at the large number of cases of supplies and the baggage that had come with Doctor Nessman; and he saw the astonishment on the faces of the natives that one so young could be a doctor.

"Good," Schweitzer said. "Then begin at once and get these men to unload the canoe."

In a few moments Schweitzer was himself astonished at the amiable but unmistakable competence with which

Albert Schweitzer

the youth handled the job of boss stevedore with a gang of workers of whose language he did not know a syllable.

Schweitzer was eager to hear news of the outside world, but he could hardly get a word out to ask Doctor Nessman, so overcome was he at having a professional colleague at last. In his journal Schweitzer wrote, "It is blissful to be able to admit to myself how tired I am."

The natives called Doctor Nessman, "the little doctor," meaning young, but their respect for him was great.

Tired though Schweitzer was, and notwithstanding the great help "the little doctor" meant to him, Schweitzer drove ahead at the strenuous program of building that was so imperative.

A seventeen-year-old native, Minkoe, whom he had cured, proved a hard worker and assistant to Schweitzer in construction work.

And after his hard day's work at the hospital itself Doctor Nessman would join them, glad to "relax" with hammer and saw.

One day soon after that the three gleefully shook hands. A building that added forty beds to the hospital was up.

Next morning Schweitzer and Minkoe went full tilt at their next objective, more huts, more beds, and more storage places for drugs and food.

Thirty more beds were added, with a good roof over

them, and they went up with speed that would have been creditable even in temperate climate.

But the demand for still more beds grew faster than the supply.

For the Benjabis, a tribe from the interior, were flocking into the region, drawn there by their poverty at home and the prospects of lumbering jobs along the Ogowé. Schweitzer described them as "homeless proletarians in the saddest sense of the word."

Coming from hills and open country, they could not take the climate of the Ogowé. The food was strange and made them ill. They did not know a word of the language. They were unused to the jungle, and it made them afraid. The work in lumbering is rugged by any standard, and the Benjabis had been used to an almost effortless existence. They had to work on floating logs, and few of them could swim. Also, they heard much about cannibals around them.

And they were very homesick.

They began to ail and flocked to the hospital. They knew nothing about Schweitzer, and they decided he was running the hospital for profit. Nor could Schweitzer or any of his native assistants make themselves in the least understood by the Benjabis.

When Schweitzer had first come to Lambaréné he had only two languages to cope with, Galoa and Pahouin. Since he had returned, the number had grown to ten; and now he had still another language, but no interpreters.

The situation took on a poignantly painful aspect one

day when a young Benjabi, beside himself with the agony of a strangulated hernia, was rushed to Schweitzer for an operation. He was almost mad with pain, but when he was laid on the operating table a look of horror came over his face, and Schweitzer saw why. The youth had been hearing about cannibalism in the region, and now that he saw knives he was sure that he had fallen into the hands of man-eaters. There was no one to tell him otherwise, and only Schweitzer's face could speak to him.

Everyone could see the choice that was in the patient's mind, the pain or the other thing. Finally exhausted, he let the anesthetic get to him. "Never have I used the operating knife with such deep emotion," Schweitzer wrote later.

Long after the youth had come out of the ether he still looked dazed, then he could not believe it, and finally his mouth trembled and a smile came.

But a primitive people finding itself in a region strange to it and in an environment even more savage than any they have known sinks to a level of confusion and disintegration that made the Benjabis seem even less developed than the tribes along the Ogowé.

They came in increasing numbers to the hospital and gave endless trouble, with their utter lack of understanding of even the simplest of obligations. They burned precious planks for firewood, they stole from the hospital hen house, and even filched food in the night from patients too weak to resist them.

Their numbers at the hospital continued to grow, and

with them came a deterioration that made Schweitzer mourn in his journal, "My hospital is no longer what it used to be."

To add to Schweitzer's troubles, both his feet became infected so badly, and resisted cure so stubbornly, that he could not walk and had to be carried down to his work every day. Had he stayed home, work on the hospital would have slowed up.

"The worst of these ulcers," he complained in his journal, "is that the burning pain causes extreme nervous irritation."

Then Doctor Nessmann came down with boils.

This threw so much work on Mathilde Kottman that at the end of a day she would sit down on the edge of her bed, struggling against tears of exhaustion.

That was their Christmas of 1924 and their new year.

30

BUT A VICTIM of sleeping sickness had been re-
sponding to treatment with the new drug that the
Rockefeller Institute had sent. Fear and torturing head-
aches were gone, and the hospital staff was "immensely
cheered." The patient had not been told what had
been the matter with him, and only now learned that
he had escaped the "killing sickness."

Then came exciting news—still another doctor was
coming to help at Lambaréné.

That was enough to set off another fever of building. There would have to be new living quarters now
that a medical staff was gathering.

A grateful Canadian whom Schweitzer had saved
from death at the hospital rounded up a work gang and
went foraging for hardwood piles. He brought back a
goodly quantity, and the villagers at N'Gomo, where
there was a saw pit, made the planks. A native carpenter, husband of a patient, helped build.

Then one day a shining new motorboat arrived, the
gift from The Friends of Lambaréné in Sweden. It

was twenty-eight feet long, five feet wide, was properly shallow of draught, could carry a ton, and had a powerful motor. In all, it was of such stuff as dreams were made of at Lambaréné. It was named *Tack sy Mycket*, Swedish for "many thanks."

Schweitzer took a two-day trip in it to answer a sick call in the distance. As he neared the landing on his return to Lambaréné, he saw a newcomer waiting for him, a "slender figure in the elegantly careless attitude of a cavalry officer."

It was Doctor Mark Lauterburg.

Within an hour Lauterburg was operating on a patient.

The natives at once dubbed him "N'Tschinda-N'Tschinda," "the man who cuts boldly."

Almost immediately he had to make a major adaptation in his attitude toward amputation, something that had been forced upon Schweitzer before him. In Europe, when amputation would save a man's life, it follows as a matter of course. But Schweitzer knew that he had a bitter choice to make. If he followed the procedure, Lambaréné would become known to the natives as the place where one loses his limbs, and few would venture there, and death would follow. He had to take risks, therefore, by not amputating.

Fortunately he had not had cause to regret his decision. His success was due partly to his skill as a surgeon, and partly to his use of methylviolet dressing. It was not long before Doctor Lauterburg was won over to Schweitzer's technique, and he became enthusiastic when he found it working in situations which would have been declared hopeless in Europe.

From Switzerland a skilled carpenter arrived, drawn there by what he had heard and read of Schweitzer's work. He was so fired with zeal, and was so superb at his work—and later as a construction boss—that Schweitzer's spirits soared.

But he hardly had had time to welcome him before Schweitzer and Doctor Nessmann had to board the *Many Thanks* and hurry to a nearby village to try to stop an epidemic of dysentery that was spreading along the Ogowé.

Schweitzer did not want it at Lambaréné.

It had been dysentery that had sent him as a patient down the long decline in health on his return to Europe. But he was, after all, a doctor and had taken every precaution possible to keep it from infecting others. Furthermore, when its consequences got beyond him, there was a noted surgeon in a modern European hospital to save him.

But if the epidemic came to Lambaréné Schweitzer knew that he would have all the trouble in the world making his native patients observe even the simplest precautions on their own behalf and that of others.

They were afraid of evil spirits, but no amount of talk would make them realize that they themselves would be spreading sickness and death by the mere neglect of cleanliness, or by touching another who had the disease.

No, Schweitzer did not want dysentery at Lambaréné, but he found a number of cases at the village so desperately ill that he had to bring them back with him.

Although he had no isolation ward he hoped somehow to cope with the cases he had brought and keep the disease from spreading. During his absence work on a new building had gone so well that Schweitzer might have succeeded in keeping dysentery from raising havoc at the hospital itself.

But the epidemic had spread so furiously throughout the region that it swept up to the hospital on the tide of new arrivals, and overwhelmed it.

Emetin, a new preparation, was a help in the treatment of the disease, but faster than help from any source was the threat of the disease itself. And again there was Schweitzer's refrain: "Unfortunately this drug is terribly expensive."

The epidemic necessitated chores of sanitation so repulsive that the natives refused to touch them, and it was the medical staff that had to attend to these chores, too, Schweitzer included.

The natives did not even take precautions with their own cooking utensils, notwithstanding the sternest of warnings. The result was that they would wash them in polluted water and catch dysentery. Or some of the water would be thrown on the ground, others would step in it, and become carriers of contagion. Beds, clothing, and other articles with which one came in contact also spread the disease.

"I ought to have isolation wards for my patients,"

Albert Schweitzer

Schweitzer mourned, "but I have not. . . . If I could only provide so much as a hut with a good strong fence around it! . . . It is useless trying to get the patients to be careful. They are told to use water only from the spring, and not from the river which is polluted, but the river is only twenty feet away, while the spring is a hundred. . . . I forbid them to do any cooking with the dysentery patients but they do it and eat out of the same dishes. . . ."

Building was going on so feverishly that Schweitzer could have more than the one hut he wanted. And he got his huts, but the tide of patients came in faster than the numbers the hospital could accommodate.

A homesick Benjabi who was there with a curable case of ulcers was seen talking animatedly with another Benjabi, who was dying of dysentery. Doctor Nessmann, who had acquired a few words of the language, rushed up to him.

"Do you want to die?" Doctor Nessmann shouted. "Get away from him."

"It is better to die," the young Benjabi said, "than not to talk with him; he's from my village."

He was dragged away, but not in time, and paid for his homesickness with his life.

What horrified the hospital staff was that patients who came there with only minor ailments were exposed to the epidemic in spite of all that a harassed and overworked staff could do.

Schweitzer, for example, came upon a sick man who had been deserted by his family and was dying of hunger. He brought him to Lambaréné, fed him up—then lost him to dysentery.

"We were all worn out and distressed," he wrote, "trying in vain to arrest the growing epidemic in the hospital. . . . Some patients who were on the point of being discharged after an operation have caught dysentery and some of them we were unable to save. . . . Now when anyone comes to me confident that I can cure him on the operating table I tremble. . . ."

In despair at the criminal negligence on the part of the natives, and worn out one day by the futile and maddening battle, Schweitzer threw himself into a chair and cried out to Joseph, "What a blockhead I was to come out here and try to cure savages!"

"Yes, Doctor," Joseph said. "Here on earth you are a blockhead. But not in heaven."

It seemed lost on Schweitzer. His written comment was, "Joseph likes to make sententious remarks like that. I wish he would be more of a help to us in keeping the epidemic down."

Only the bad temper of an overworked man could account for the comment. In fact, Schweitzer himself told how, just at about this time, Joseph returned from mourning the death of his mother and had cut short the prescribed period of its observation in order to get back to Lambaréné in its critical need of every last bit of help it could get.

"The Doctor is a slave to work," was his explanation, "and I am a slave to the Doctor."

What may have also hurried him back was another calamity which was advancing on Lambaréné. Famine was on the march.

31

IT REACHED Lambaréné in the fall of 1925. Schweitzer had foreseen it. It was largely due to a lack of the rice which traders imported to supplement the insufficient food crops of the region. They had overestimated the banana and manioc crops, which failed that year, so they had not bought enough rice from abroad. Then several shiploads of rice were wrecked.

Schweitzer had wisely stored up more than enough for his hospital. But now that the whole region was starving, and falling sick, he had no choice but to share some of his stock with others outside of Lambaréné. But he had about one hundred and fifty mouths to

feed, and he had to make some heartrending refusals.

Several times he found himself with only enough food supply for several days, but each time by super-human effort and with the help of *Many Thanks* he was able to save the situation. There was an understand-able give-and-take between the hospital and some of the traders. But he was wondering if he would not have to close the hospital and send his patients away.

And this was only one of the many problems that haunted Schweitzer day and night at this time.

He must stamp out the epidemic . . . but since he could not he must see to it that never again would he be found defenseless against a repetition of it. . . . He must see to it that never again would famine threaten those who came to him to be healed. . . . He must see to this . . . he must see to that . . . until the mount-ing demands gave him no rest, and now he could no longer dispense with rest at night. . . . Nor could he afford the luxury of despair and defeat.

Early one morning he stole off by himself to a hill-side a mile and three-quarters upstream from Lam-baréné. The Ogowé divides at that point into two branches. The spacious valley where he stood, between the jungle and the river, had once been the site of two villages, and clearing the land would not be quite the laborious undertaking it would have been had the jungle remained there untouched.

Without telling anyone of the errand that was tak-ing him away from Lambaréné, Schweitzer went to see

the District Commissioner. Schweitzer told him of his project and obtained the concession of about two hundred acres of the land he had inspected. Then he returned to Lambaréné.

That night he called his staff together and told them that the situation at the hospital was so hopeless that it was useless to try to cope with it the way things stood, and that he had taken the first steps to set up a new hospital on grounds he had just obtained.

There would be isolation wards that would enable them to deal with the dysentery epidemic and any other that might come. And enough land would be under cultivation to make the hospital self-sufficient in the way of food, no matter what famine conditions there might be elsewhere.

For some moment there was the silence of shocked surprise and realization of what it all meant. Then the natives in the hospital and the workers at the mission were startled by jubilant cries and cheers at the doctors' headquarters.

The staff stayed up late that night, too excited to sleep. Finally, however, Schweitzer was alone; he needed to be. He had a painful personal adjustment to make. It had been two-and-a-half years since he had seen his family, and he had promised to rejoin them by that time.

Now, even with the best of luck, it would be at least a year more before the new hospital would be ready. But if he went off to Europe—even if he could get himself to leave Lambaréné at such a time—there would be no work done on the new hospital.

So he sat down and wrote his wife that it would be at least another year before he could come home.

32

EVERY morning some of the work gang headed by Schweitzer left the hospital in canoes, paddled two miles, and got out on the new site. Others followed in the *Many Thanks*.

Men have used different devices to keep from thinking of some overwhelmingly laborious present and future, and Schweitzer conceived a day with his work gangs in the form of a symphony.

In the first movement "the men very grumpily take up their axes and bushknives and proceed in snail-like tempo to the part of the jungle to be cleared."

In the second movement "the conductor tries in vain

to quicken the very moderate tempo in which the cutting goes on. Not a breath of air is stirring."

"The scherzo comes with a little gust of wind that steals up from the river." Schweitzer cracks a joke or two, there is laughter, "the human atmosphere gets livelier, merry words fly here and there, and a few begin to sing." The work picks up a little.

In the finale, Schweitzer has managed to work them up into the feeling that the jungle is their mortal enemy and here is their chance to get at it. "Wild imprecations are hurled at it, they charge at it with howls and yells, and slash away with bushknives and axes."

But the conductor is praying that no distraction occurs, no matter how slight, not a bird whirring out of the brush, nor the sight of a squirrel, not even a word from the conductor. Otherwise the spell of fury is broken, "axes and bushknives come to rest and there will be no getting them back into the mood again."

The end comes suddenly with the call from the conductor, "Amani, amani!", "Enough, enough!" and the work on the clearing stops for the day.

Schweitzer may have found the satisfactory art form to describe a day's work by the natives. He would have been hard put to it to describe his own, there were so many levels of consciousness active at the same time.

Even his eyes were taking in several things at once: the speed of the approaching storm; how the work was going; watching the ground to see that no sudden slithering movement in the underbrush found his men unprepared; and glancing every so often in the direction of the hospital on the lookout for a hurry call.

At the same time his mind was shuttling between the clearing and the hospital, thinking of this patient or another, and worrying as much about his staff. This one is definitely overworking even by Schweitzer's standards; another *must* be made to slow down, too; a third is showing symptoms disturbing to a doctor. Yes, the epidemic was telling on his workers, too. . . .

And notwithstanding his lifelong passion of concentration on whatever he was doing at the time, his thoughts also shuttled between Africa and Europe. Irresistibly, visions of his family came. When would he see them? . . . And his friends in Europe, would they be able to find the funds for his imperatively ambitious program? . . .

Also, as in some richly complicated orchestral passage, themes and subthemes came to the forefront, some darting into awareness for a moment only, others not appearing in the consciousness at all but coloring the whole as an underlying mood.

For in spite of all his efforts not to think of a cataclysmic future at a time when he was straining every nerve and resource in building, he saw skies darkening all over the world.

An egomaniac in Italy was in power there, fancied himself a Caesar, and was readying his armies for conquest in Africa. . . . Another in Germany, far surpassing him in danger, was also planning conquest. After he had captured Germany—and he seemed on the way to it—he was planning to take the world. . . .

In Japan, their counterpart, the military rulers, were out to conquer Asia. . . . Only war could come of it all. . . .

But whenever this theme threatened to dominate Schweitzer's thoughts he took refuge in strenuous muscular action. Every building in the new hospital village would have to stand on piles, to keep snakes from wandering in and to let the flood waters from the river and the rainy season torrents sweep under the buildings instead of taking them along.

The piles had to be so carefully placed that Schweitzer had to set every one himself. "Often I have to push the heavy pile just a centimeter or two to get it into the right position . . . and I must get down into the post hole myself, put my arms about it and move it as required. If all goes well I can get a dozen piles placed in a day."

But inevitably, too, the firmer he got a set of supports fixed the more the thought must have flashed through him, would the new hospital fare any better in a world-wide storm than his first had done? . . .

However, even his many-faceted mind was too busy by day to give such questions more than a moment's involuntary thought.

For among his problems he had constantly to make compromises that would have brought gray hairs to an ordinary builder. In cutting down trees, for instance, he let piles of logs remain on the grounds of the hospital-to-be for firewood. "Unfortunately they provide a good home for snakes, but we have no choice. Any-

Genius in the Jungle

how there are so many on our grounds already that a few hundred more make little difference."

He rounded up enough hardwood beams but could not get them sawed. It took a lumber dealer's misfortune—his wife was desperately ill—to solve that problem. Schweitzer saved her, and the grateful husband sent him a crew of sawyers.

Other help, even more important, came from Europe. Mlle. Martha Lauterburg, Dr. Lauterburg's sister, arrived from Alsace and became a godsend to the hospital.

A young Swiss builder, Kurt Muggensturm, came, and Schweitzer wrote, "Now I can breathe, though not quite freely."

The young Swiss proved to be a competent overseer, and Schweitzer was able to go off on trips to gather more lumber without the worry that all work would stop in his absence.

A Frenchman, M. Gonne, also helped in supervising the work.

Dr. Nessmann had to return to Europe, but in his place came Dr. Trensz, son of an Alsace pastor. In the course of his struggle with the epidemic he made a discovery in the field of dysentery that became a contribution to tropical medicine.

Schweitzer, too, tried out a new drug on himself that freed him from the tortures of his infected feet and became part of the medicine kit of every European who came to Lambaréné.

By this time Schweitzer had set the piles for the

whole hospital village. The walls of three parallel lines of buildings began to go up. Every building was long and narrow and ran east and west to get a minimum of equatorial sun. Roofs went on, not of perishable grass tiles but of good corrugated iron.

The plantation was already partly cultivated and was delivering its first crop of cabbages and beans. But exceptionally high river waters swept part of the land away and some of the first crop was lost. That meant more work building up the bank at the flooded section, in all of which Schweitzer took on more than his share of the manual labor.

Evenings found him in no condition to work on his book on St. Paul. But no matter how exhausted, he always put in some time at the zinc-lined piano. It was no longer only a matter of escape or refreshment of the spirit that took him there. He also had to keep his fingers in condition for the time when he would be working for the hospital at concerts in Europe.

But when the hour became too late for playing he could no longer escape the thoughts that he had managed to drive off during the day.

All day long he had to decide what is small and what is not. A dysentery germ, for instance, is certainly small, yet Schweitzer strained his eyes peering at it through a microscope at a time when he had to shut out of his mind the million Nazis Hitler had recruited in the last six months.

Schweitzer spent sleepless nights and used up a precious new drug on a patient with sleeping sickness; the outcome of this might be the hope that countless other sufferers would be saved. At the same time he had to turn back two tragic madmen to certain death, because there was no room for them at the hospital.

He would have made no move to brush off a harmless ant, even though it was stinging him, yet every morning he turned his back on the patients dying of the epidemic and went off to pound piles two miles away. . . .

But at night Hitler's gains came back to Schweitzer's thoughts. The madmen Schweitzer had sent away now haunted him. And in bed he could not turn his back on the epidemic. . . .

He blamed himself for not having planned on a large enough scale from the first, to withstand both epidemic and famine. There should have been isolation wards enough, and plantation enough before he undertook to see his first patient. . . . And it is elementary that an epidemic had best be treated at the source. There must be outpost hospitals. . . .

He had thought of his plantation as the Garden of Eden. "Some day there must be enough fruit and food growing on our own grounds so that anybody will be able to take as much as he pleases, and there will be no such thing as stealing."

But what is the use of staving off hunger at the hospital when famine in the region around undermines the health of its inhabitants and sends so many more sick to the hospital? . . . No, he must cut deeper and deeper into the jungle and reclaim more and more of it for cultivation. . . . But a plantation cut out of the jungle would have no mere struggle against temperate zone weeds, bugs, birds, and small animals. Parasites would creep out of the jungle that had already strangled great trees. There would be locust plagues and traveler ants. And along the Ogowé, plantations had to cope with herds of wild elephants. . . .

That meant border patrols for his plantations . . . big staffs of doctors and nurses . . . and prodigious labor. . . . And there he was, planning all this, at a time when it was questionable if his health would even outlast the completion of the hospital he was building. For he knew now that his more than three years of Africa without a break and without a rest had made him a sick man again. . . .

Yet even on steaming, stifling nights, when sleep would not come and black thoughts did, Schweitzer found help in thinking of the man who long before him had lived in the same room at the Old Fish Market in Strasbourg where Schweitzer had spent student days. He thought of the last part of Goethe's greatest drama, where Faust finds inner peace at last through vast labor, wresting from the sea land on which, and by which, men could live. Only with Schweitzer it was the jungle instead of the sea.

> Below the hills a marshy plain
> Infects what I so long have been retrieving;
> The stagnant pool likewise to drain
> Will be my latest and my best achieving.

Genius in the Jungle

To many . . . let me furnish soil
Though not secure, yet free to active toil . . .
Yes, to this thought I hold with firm persistence.
Only he earns his freedom and existence
Who daily conquers them anew. . . .

When such lines passed through Schweitzer's mind they must have been as tangible a man-to-man communion as any whisper in the dark.

"And thus was Goethe at my side in the swampy forest," Schweitzer wrote. "A man who really understood."

33

ON THE morning of January 21, 1927, there was pleasant excitement on the river for miles up and downstream from Lambaréné. White traders and natives, former patients and the families and friends of the patients now at the hospital had come in motorboats and canoes to help move the patients from the old hospital to the new.

Everyone was wearing smiles and his Sunday best. The day was brilliant and for once not too hot. The river sparkled. A breeze fluttered the flags and colored streamers with which some of the river craft were decked. The *Many Thanks*, as was fitting for the flag-ship of a fleet, was gayest of all.

Doctor Trensz was away on an emergency call up the river, but Doctor Lauterburg, his sister, and Nurse Hausknecht, assisted by native orderlies and others, helped or carried those patients who could not walk by themselves down to the canoes and motorboats.

Headed by the *Many Thanks*, a procession of river craft loaded with patients set off amid cheers for the new hospital. There Nurse Kottman and Kurt Mug-gensturm helped the patients to the new quarters.

All day a procession of river craft ferried between the old hospital and the new. In the middle of the after-noon a European couple arrived at the new hospital just in time for the woman to give birth to her baby. Schweitzer was happy that he was now well-prepared for "such tricks of fate," as he put it.

By evening there was only one more group of pa-tients to bring over, and Schweitzer took charge of them himself. They were the insane. He took charge not only because he could handle them best, but also because they touched him so profoundly, these men and women who lived in darkness and in multiplying fears until it all became too much for them.

Genius in the Jungle

They had been living in mere cages on damp earth, the best he had been able to do for them. Now they were told there would be comfortable quarters for them with floors of wood, and they were waiting to see their new home with the impatience of overeager children.

That night Schweitzer heard with profound emotion a refrain that ran from ward to ward.

"It's a good hut, Doctor, a good hut!"

But the voices that touched him most came from the insane ward. "Yes, Doctor, it *is* a good hut!"

Schweitzer was busy the next few days at the deserted old hospital retrieving every precious plank, every bit of corrugated iron, even bent nails that could be hammered straight, they were all so hard to replace.

For several nights one of the nurses saw Schweitzer leave his room at two in the morning and stand at different spots on the new hospital grounds. He was studying what adjustments to make to give the patients the full benefit of the river breeze that came up at this time.

Doctor Trensz had to return to Europe.

But on March 23, Doctor Ernest Mundler, a Swiss, arrived to take his place.

With him came an Englishwoman, Mrs. C. E. B. Russell, who had acted as interpreter to Schweitzer in England and had translated several of his books into English. Schweitzer met her with a gift, a motherless baby monkey. Mrs. Russell later wrote a charming book, *My Monkey Friends,* and the dedication ran: "To Doctor Albert Schweitzer, who teaches reverence for life, and who has saved many a little orphan, human and subhuman, from misery and destruction."

One of her first questions of Schweitzer was how she was to act with the natives until she got her own bearings.

"Just imagine that you are a shepherd dog," he smiled. She found her flock most willing to be shepherded. Schweitzer wrote: "It had been my experience on the whole that the natives obey a white woman better than they do us men."

She took his place even in such strenuous projects as clearing the jungle.

And she became his chief aide with the insane.

Soon after her arrival, for instance, a canoe full of agitated Pahouins drew up at the new hospital, bringing a giant native in chains. Schweitzer and Mrs. Russell were waiting for them at the landing. They already knew that N'Tschambi, the man in chains, had killed a woman in a fit of madness. As he sat in the canoe his face showed even greater agitation than those who had brought him.

Schweitzer reached down, helped him to the landing, and took a long look at the man's face. It was clear that N'Tschambi was afraid, like the others, of himself.

The overlay of fear on his face, however, did not hide the basic sadness in it, and the sensitiveness that had made him so easy a prey to all the terrors of the jungle world.

Nature had been cruel to him in an inverted way. She had given him a rugged body, thus denying him the mercy of some easy death. She had endowed him with exceptional sensitivity, as if to make sure that he would not escape the least of the torments that was in store for him. And in a world where the savage temper is a vital weapon of survival she had given him instead a craving for kindness and as great a need to live by it himself. It showed in the very modeling of his face.

"Take off these chains," Schweitzer ordered.

He had to do it himself, the others were so afraid.

N'Tschambi was all the more bewildered when Schweitzer and Mrs. Russell drew their arms through his and walked him up the hill.

At the hospital Schweitzer explained to him what sedatives would do and asked if he wanted some. N'Tschambi nodded, and in a short while he became calmer.

He was given one of the new rooms in the insane ward, quieted down noticeably, and that night slept for the first time without nightmares.

He became a model patient. Schweitzer, who was studying him closely, soon gave him brief periods of freedom about the hospital grounds. But the fear that N'Tschambi saw in other faces agitated him, and he would return to his room voluntarily.

But freedom from fear came more often and lasted longer, especially when Schweitzer gave him odd jobs to do around the hospital. On such occasions N'Tschambi attacked the work, whatever it was, with a fierce energy that made all but Schweitzer and Mrs. Russell uneasy.

Then one day Schweitzer took him to a grindstone and gave him an ax. "I've got some clearing to do in the woods," he said, "and I want you to come and help me. But the ax is dull. I wish you would sharpen it for me."

N'Tschambi drew back in alarm.

"What's the matter?" Schweitzer asked.

"I don't want to touch it!" N'Tschambi said. "I'm afraid."

"Of what?"

"What I might do."

Schweitzer grew impatient. "If I'm not afraid, why should you be? Come on, we're wasting time."

The whole hospital watched as Schweitzer went off into the jungle with N'Tschambi at his back, carrying an ax.

Hours later they returned, N'Tschambi's big body dripping with sweat and obviously exhausted. But there was a radiant smile on his lips.

In time the hospital became accustomed to seeing N'Tschambi work by himself, or in Mrs. Russell's work gang clearing the jungle with bushknife and ax. No one equalled him for sustained, untiring labor.

And one day the whole hospital saw Mrs. Russell go off on a clearing job with only N'Tschambi to help her, and he was carrying the ax.

He stayed on at Lambaréné as a worker. Only at rare intervals did he ask to be locked up, and even these periods did not last.

Genius in the Jungle

Meanwhile the dysentery patients had been isolated in the big building and were so fenced off from the rest of the hospital that supervision over them became effective.

The result was that one day the count of dysentery patients showed the first decline since the start of the epidemic. The decline continued, until at last the number of patients in the isolation ward was no greater than normal.

Even the famine throughout the region abated at this time.

By July Schweitzer was gloating. "The big pile-built village has quite a dignified look," he wrote. "And how much easier the work is now, for at last we have space enough, air enough in our wards, and light enough. How delighted we all feel. . . ."

A number of native babies whose mothers had died in childbirth were being kept on at the hospital. The place was taking on a domestic look.

Schweitzer could leave Lambaréné now with the knowledge that there were two doctors, two nurses, and five native orderlies remaining.

On July 21, 1927, the whole hospital, the mission, and neighbors saw Schweitzer, Mathilde Kottman, and Nurse Lauterburg off for Europe.

The last to say good-by was N'Tschambi, who came to Schweitzer in tears. "Doctor," he pleaded, "have you given orders that no one can send me away while you are in Europe?"

Schweitzer smiled. "Certainly, N'Tschambi, no one can send you away without first having a big palaver with me."

And Mrs. Russell, remaining behind, added her smile of assurance to Schweitzer's.

part five

———

34

IT WAS on board ship that Schweitzer felt the full impact of whatever was the matter with his health this time. The doctors would soon tell him what was specifically wrong with him, so he put off thinking about it.

But he was nearing Europe, he would be in Germany in a few days, and the doctor who was diagnosing an ailing civilization and worried about all his patients could not help thinking of the world in general and of Europe in particular.

For it seemed that the statesmen who were in the seats of power disagreed with Schweitzer's diagnosis that the most devastating war in history was in the making.

For them and for millions who thought like them there was a rainbow of hope arching over the world, the League of Nations. Even Germany had been admitted to it, and the man at the head of the nation that had most reason to fear that country, Aristide Briand, Premier of France, was the one who most warmly welcomed it.

"No more war!" he exclaimed ecstatically. "No more shall we resort to brutal and sanguinary methods to settle our disputes. Henceforth . . . just as individual citizens take their difficulties to be settled by a magistrate, so shall we bring ours to be settled by pacific procedure."

Chancellor of Germany, Gustave Stresemann, perhaps less ecstatic, was just as relieved. "Only he realizes that the sea is smooth who has seen it stirred up by the tempest," he said.

In 1926 the two men jointly received the Nobel Peace Prize for their "achievements in bringing peace to Europe."

But Schweitzer must have seen, not a healing of the world's wounds but a growing focus of infection in Germany, of which he was a citizen and where he was soon due.

Even a weak government would have hanged a man who had tried to overthrow it, as Hitler had attempted in 1923. But Germany was worse than weak, it was already too ill either to throw off Hitler or his movement. For his high crime he merely was sentenced to "five years of honorable detention" and was allowed to go free at the end of six months.

Schweitzer's thoughts must have been on Hitler not only because of what the man would mean to the world, but also because in all Germany there could not have been two men whose lives, innate drives, and overall outlooks were so violently in conflict. Their ways of life could not co-exist, except in separated and limited areas, but neither man was content with less than the whole world for the scope of his operations.

How inevitable it was that the two should come in conflict may be seen even in their childhoods. There was Schweitzer's boyhood, and there was the glimpse that Hitler gives of his own in *Mein Kampf*. He wrote of his "companionships with unusually robust boys, which at times caused my mother much grief. . . . I had become a little ringleader and for obvious reasons my father could not appreciate the talent of his quarrelsome son."

Then, too, there was Schweitzer's early and continuing success in almost everything he had touched, even in his student days; whereas in Hitler's case there was failure at everything except in those projects in which hatred was an asset.

The outbreak of the world war in 1914 was horrifying proof to Schweitzer of his diagnosis that civilization was decaying. When Hitler heard that war had broken out, "I fell on my knees and thanked heaven from my overflowing heart."

Albert Schweitzer

At the time Briand and Stresemann were hailing a new era of peace, Hitler's propaganda meetings were growing bigger and more turbulent. In *Mein Kampf* he wrote about the way his men dealt with those who disagreed with what they heard on the speaker's platform. "My Storm Troopers in groups of eight and ten attacked them. Scarcely a minute passed without my seeing the hecklers bloody and maimed. Suddenly a wild shooting started. It was my men, and my heart jubilated with such awakening of old war memories . . ."

It seems almost incredible that in the same land a Schweitzer could be pleading for reverence for life, and a Goebbels, Hitler's propaganda chief and speaking for him, could be cheered by masses of Germans as Goebbels shouted: "We shall reach our goal when we have the courage to laugh as we destroy, as we smash whatever has been sacred to us as tradition, as education and human affection."

Friends of Schweitzer's, knowing how he felt about the growth of Hitler's power, urged him to join the movement against it. Schweitzer had not the least talent for the thousand and one tricks and techniques of power politics, ranging as they do from character assassination to assassination with knife and gun.

But with Germany as Schweitzer's home and with the drive of his philosophy it was inevitable that the two men should one day come into collision.

35

IN STRASBOURG doctors examined Schweitzer and gave him emphatic orders. No lectures, no concerts, rest.

Because his wife's health still required altitude, Schweitzer bought a small house at Königsfeld amid the pines and mountains of the Black Forest. It was simple to the point of rusticity, and often when Schweitzer worked at night in his room on the top floor he could hear even a mouse nibbling in the basement.

But he could also hear the sleepy sound of treetops and the notes of a nightingale, and now he did not have to shut them out as memories that made a present painful by contrast.

He drank in deep draughts of joy of being with his wife, of giving his daughter her first piano lessons, and for a brief period he did obey his doctors and stayed home.

But how brief it was may be seen from the fact that during the first six weeks of his return he spent only three nights at Königsfeld.

Albert Schweitzer

His first problem was to send replacements to Lambaréné, as several of his staff had to return to Europe. His new volunteers were Doctors Mundler, Hediger, Stalder, and Schnabel, all from Switzerland. A fifth, Dr. Eric Dölken, died of a heart attack on the voyage to Lambaréné. How hard Schweitzer took the news may be well imagined.

Meanwhile, instead of the needed sleep the doctors had prescribed, he worked on his book on St. Paul often till six in the morning, allowing himself only four hours sleep a day.

He also stole off to Holland to perform the marriage ceremony for the son of an old friend. Then he went to England to thank his friends there for their help to his hospital.

There is a revealing glimpse of him at this point at the home of Dr. Maude Royden, the famous preacher, one of the English friends of Lambaréné. Her written account of him describes "the terrific impact of his presence indoors, with a riot of people surging around him; secretaries with their typewriters relegated to the bathroom and the stairs; important and importunate callers, all demanding interviews with him. . . ."

When Schweitzer was leaving, Miss Royden spoke of the honor she and her household had felt in having had him as their guest. At the word honor Schweitzer, gravely shocked, drew her aside and beseeched her never to use the word again in such a connection with him.

But in the fall of the year he received an expression

Genius in the Jungle

of honor which he could not rebuke, nor could he refuse to accept it. The city of Frankfort, birthplace of Goethe, annually awarded a prize to the individual who in their judgment had performed the most signal service to humanity. In selecting a candidate for the award Frankfort also looked for that quality in its candidates that would most reflect the many-sidedness of Goethe, as well as his spirit and philosophy.

The prize was substantial financially and still more sought after because of the high honor accorded to it by Germans in all walks of life.

In the course of the ceremonies Schweitzer's speech was a glowing tribute to Goethe, whose disciple he humbly considered himself.

For sheer Olympian genius Goethe was, of course, one of the greatest in history. But for greatness of humanity and service to some of its most miserable masses, Schweitzer had already proven himself by far the greater human being.

And he had far more faith in humanity than Goethe had felt.

With the easy generosity of youth, for instance, Goethe had urged that the great estates of the rich be cut up for the benefit of the people. But in time he gave it up as a dream. "We are sure in our younger days that we can build palaces for mankind," he wrote. "But with experience we find that the most we can do is to clean up their dunghills."

Few men have known so well as Schweitzer what it means to clean up dunghills for suffering humanity. Yet

213

after many years of grim and revolting experience with it he had a more heartening message than Goethe's.

He urged youth "to hold fast, their whole life through, to the thoughts and emotions that inspire them. It is through the idealism of youth that man catches sight of the truth, and in that idealism he possesses riches which he must never exchange for anything else."

The spreading fame of Lambaréné brought so many people to consult with Schweitzer that the storey-and-a-half cabin in Königsfeld proved inadequate. Schweitzer also wanted to build a rest home for those of his Lambaréné workers who had had too much of Africa at one time and needed recuperation.

With the substantial sum that the Goethe prize had brought him he decided to build such a rest home, and to combine it with a home for himself.

There was only one place that he could think of as his lifetime home, the village in which he was born and had been brought up, and whose earth and sky and air would always be dear to him.

It had to be Günsbach.

His father had died, and the parsonage could no longer be the roof for Schweitzer except as an honored guest.

In hunting for a location for his new home Schweitzer showed a degree of choosiness that mystified some of his friends. There was no lack of pleasant sites for homes in Günsbach, and the one Schweitzer finally chose did not seem strikingly superior to those he had turned down. It was on a promontory of rocks, the *Rochers de Känzenrain*, where as a boy he would sit and dream as he looked up the valley to Münster and the peaks of the Vosges. Friends suggested that he build his house in back of a garden to insure privacy. But Schweitzer wanted it to be a "house by the side of the road," symbolic of his feeling as "a friend to man."

He designed the house himself and called in a Colmar architect only to help in working out the details. It blended the lines of the ancient Günsbach houses with streamlined modern architecture.

Germany was so poor that Schweitzer had felt it unfair to take the Goethe prize money out of the country. He solved the problem by giving concerts and lectures in Germany until the money these brought equalled the Goethe prize, then he donated the proceeds to German charities.

Notwithstanding his disobedience of the doctor's orders to rest, Schweitzer had been rushing, as one friend reported, "from one city to another, often by night, always without comfort, and always third class if no fourth class was available."

It was not niggardliness that made Schweitzer economize, but every dollar he might have spent on what he considered comfort he saved instead for necessities of life at Lambaréné.

The only times he did not practice such austerity was when his wife was with him.

He gave organ recitals and lectures in England and on the continent. In between times he was busy in his little office in Strasbourg, which had become the clearing house for all matters concerning Lambaréné. He went to Czechoslovakia, as the guest of President Masaryk.

In spite of his need for rest he became his old buoyant, dynamic self, so that everyone who came in contact with him thought that here was a man who found the present good and the future promising.

But an intimate friend finally asked him why he had chosen that particular site for his guest house at Günsbach. The answer was shocking.

"I want to build here," Schweitzer said, "because the house will be under the hillside where the guns of the next war will not reach it."

The Guest House was begun while Schweitzer was in Europe, but he had to leave it before it was finished, for he had received disturbing news from Lambaréné.

Another dysentery epidemic had overwhelmed the new hospital, so that even the quarters of the insane had to be taken over to house the many stricken with the sickness.

Schweitzer arranged immediately to return to Africa, and this time his wife went with him.

They left their daughter in the care of a famous school maintained in Königsfeld by the Moravian Brothers, a sect whose religion was so human and universal that even the barbarous elements in decaying Germany left them in peace.

The Schweitzers sailed for Africa on the day after Christmas, 1930.

36

DETERMINED to complete his oft-interrupted work on St. Paul, and perhaps to keep from thinking of what awaited him at Lambaréné, Schweitzer worked on the book on board ship, finished it, and wrote the introduction just as the steamer reached Lambaréné.

Mrs. Schweitzer was deeply touched by the outpouring of welcome to her and her husband. Then she stared at the new hospital with much the same wonder and delight that was in her husband's face when he saw his daughter after an absence of nearly four years.

Fortunately along with the warm welcome to the Schweitzers good news awaited them. The dysentery epidemic had been checked, and the situation at the hospital was well in hand by the time Schweitzer took hold.

But for Schweitzer a situation that was well in hand meant that he had to plunge into more work than ever.

A new home went up for the mental cases, with room lighter and airier than before, and with a recreation room in the building. N'Tschambi, who was no

Albert Schweitzer

longer a patient but had stayed on at the hospital to help, did the work of five on the new ward for the insane.

One new building of concrete provided a dining hall and a general gathering place for the medical staff. Other structures and storage sheds were added, as well as new quarters for the hospital orderlies.

A large reservoir of concrete was built to store rain water.

Finally, financed by friends of Lambaréné, an operating room was fitted up "with everything necessary." "Now it is fine to be working at Lambaréné." Schweitzer rejoiced, "the more so since we have enough doctors and nurses, so that we do not have to work ourselves to exhaustion."

It gave him all the more time to devote himself to a deeper kind of healing.

As the hospital was now two miles away from the Mission, Schweitzer inaugurated simple religious services on his own grounds.

At nine o'clock every Sunday morning a hospital orderly went through the different wards ringing a bell. The patients, their families and friends, orderlies and staff gathered in the promenade between two rows of hospital buildings.

A phonograph played a hymn.

Then Schweitzer appeared, a Pahouin on one side of him, a Benjabi on the other.

Schweitzer spoke a sentence or two at a time in French, and paused for the Pahouin and the Bendjabi

Genius in the Jungle

to translate. His delivery was earnest but quiet. His translators were dramatic, eyes rolling, faces working, their whole bodies involved in their renditions of Schweitzer's message.

But it would be hard to imagine a more informal setting for religious services. Some of the congregation cooked their dinners while listening. A mother washed and combed her baby's hair. Men mended their fishing nets. Sheep and goats roamed about. Weaver birds, Schweitzer's pets, made so much noise in the trees that he had to raise his voice. Schweitzer also insisted that Mrs. Russell's pet monkeys be allowed to run free on Sundays, and during the services they performed gymnastics in the nearest palm trees, or jumped about on the roofs of nearby buildings until they became exhausted and settled down on Mrs. Russell's shoulders to rest.

Schweitzer's sermons were as informal as their setting.

A typical one had forgiveness for its text: "Scarcely are you up in the morning and standing in front of your hut, when somebody whom everybody knows is a bad man comes and insults you. Because the Lord Jesus says that one should forgive, you keep silent instead of beginning a palaver.

"Later on your neighbor's goat eats the bananas on which you were counting for your dinner. Instead of starting a quarrel with the neighbor you only remind him that it was his goat that was at fault, and that it would be only right if he made it up to you in bananas.

But if he insists that the goat was not his, you go off quietly and reflect that God makes so many bananas grow in your plantation that there is no need for you to begin a quarrel on that account.

"A little later a man comes to whom you gave ten bunches of bananas to sell in the market along with his. He brings you the money for only nine. You say, 'That's too little.' But he retorts, 'You made a mistake in counting, you only gave me nine bunches.' You are about to call him a liar. But then you can't help thinking about many lies for which God has to forgive *you*, so you go quietly into your hut.

"When you want to light your fire you discover that somebody has carried off the wood that you had brought from the forest yesterday. But again you'll find it in your heart to forgive whoever it is, and you don't go searching your neighbors' huts to see who had taken your wood. . . .

"Now you go home, happy and proud that you have succeeded in making yourself forgive several times. But if the Lord Jesus were to come to your village that day and you were to come to him and think he would praise you for it before all the people, he would say to you instead, as he said to Peter . . . that you must forgive again and again, and many more times before God can forgive your many sins. . . ."

In words and works Schweitzer was thus trying to teach the natives along the Ogowé an alternative to the savage way of life.

Genius in the Jungle

With the years it became clear that some of them were learning this alternative from him.

But so was Schweitzer learning. When he had first arrived in Africa, for instance, he had written that the natives were "magnificently lazy." Now he wrote: "I can no longer talk ingenuously of the laziness of the Negro after seeing fifteen of them, for instance, row upstream uninterruptedly thirty-six hours to bring a man to me who was seriously ill."

At first, too, it had seemed to him that gratitude on the part of the natives was rare. Then he began to record one instance after another that told different stories.

One native, none too prosperous, had scraped together what was for him a considerable amount of money and gave it to Schweitzer "for the expensive thread with which you sewed up my belly."

Another had been given up for dead by his family when he was sent off to Lambaréné. A few weeks later he returned to his village, and his friends and family expected him to stay and rest. But the man had come back for the sole purpose of repaying Schweitzer. He piloted a goat a hundred miles through the jungle back to Lambaréné, and left the animal as his contribution to the hospital's milk supply.

N'Tsama was recovering from the sleeping sickness, thanks to new discoveries in drugs and techniques in curing it. He was still little more than a skeleton, but one day he managed to crawl down to the river bank to sit there and fish. Schweitzer and a work gang were unloading planks nearby. Schweitzer called out, "Hey, N'Tsama, how about giving us a hand?"

He was joking, of course, and the work gang laughed.

But N'Tsama slowly rose, picked up a plank, and managed to hoist it to his shoulders.

There was a moment of surprised silence, then cheers came, not only because a man was recovering from the "killing sickness." It was also a tribute to a spirit which formerly the natives would not have understood, but which now they found exciting.

A few days later N'Tsama asked to be allowed to help in clearing the jungle, fairly strenuous work. "The Doctor is my father," he explained, "and the hospital is my village."

Even of the Benjabis, with whom Schweitzer had once had so much trouble, he now wrote, "I dare say we should have fewer difficulties with them if we could occasionally sit around a fire and show them that we were not merely medicine men and officers of the law. . . ."

Natives used to stare at Schweitzer when they saw him go to the trouble of scooping ants and frogs out of a hole in the ground that was about to be filled. It was to avoid hurting them. He tried to explain a reverence of life to natives in a world where even human life was far from sacred. But at first all he saw in the faces of his listeners was blankness, even embarrassment at what seemed to them excessive softness.

Then one day two of his work gang were cutting

away some brush when one of them saw a frog and raised his bushknife to kill it. But the other stopped him, saying, "All living creatures are the children of God and it is a sin to kill needlessly."

"He was the last man," Schweitzer wrote, "I would have expected to be affected by anything I had said."

But the most vivid lesson Schweitzer learned was from one of the natives who had at one time been an interpreter at his Sunday sermons.

Oyembo—the name means "song"—was a Galoa youth who was so intelligent and co-operative that the Mission had given him an education in the hope that he would devote his life to teaching the natives.

When Schweitzer first arrived in Lambaréné, Oyembo was teaching there, a married man with a wife and children to support on the little that the Mission could afford to pay him.

Nevertheless he stayed on, and in addition volunteered to interpret Schweitzer's Sunday sermons. Unlike the other interpreters, Oyembo would come to Schweitzer the night before and ask to hear the sermon, to prepare himself to translate it all the better the next morning.

Schweitzer had high hopes for him. Oyembo's classmates, taking advantage of the education they had received, had gone off to cash in on it in other occupations. But Oyembo had stayed on at Lambaréné.

There came a time, however, when he could no longer support his family on what the Mission could pay him, and Oyembo gave up teaching and went into the timber trade.

Schweitzer did not blame him, but every time he passed the boys' school at the Mission where Oyembo used to teach he felt a pang at what he considered a lost leader.

On one of his returns from Europe Schweitzer met Oyembo at Cape Lopez. He had been told that Oyembo had made considerable money, and it seemed to Schweitzer that the man had changed. There must have been a cutting edge to Schweitzer's tone as he said, "Well, Oyembo, you seem to be on the way to becoming a rich man."

"I'm doing pretty well," the man said quietly.

Schweitzer put him down as a deep disappointment, and said so in conversations with missionaries and traders.

Whereupon he learned something new about human nature.

He heard, for example, the story of a trader who was traveling up the Ogowé in a flat-bottomed boat laden with cases and bales of merchandise. A storm came up, and it looked as though any moment the river would overturn the boat and scatter the cargo. And none of the native crew could swim.

Only a canoe of exceptional size could rescue them, and there were few such boats in the region.

To the trader's amazement a huge canoe put out from shore, and not only saved the trader and the na-

Genius in the Jungle

tives, but the rescuers went to the trouble of fishing the bales and boxes out of the river.

The trader and his crew were brought to one of the most prosperous villages they had ever seen. The leader of the rescue party put him up at his home, exceptionally good-looking and modern.

In the morning the trader told his host how grateful he was, and when about to leave he asked how much he owed the rescuers for their services.

"Nothing," said his host. "We've only done our duty."

It was Oyembo.

Yes, Oyembo had become wealthy, but he had taken his fellow villagers into partnership with him. Their timber company, under Oyembo's direction, had adopted modern business methods, effective lumbering techniques, and had acquired a reputation that drew more and more customers to them.

Oyembo had also organized his fellow villagers into clearing a big plantation and sowing it with plantains and cassava. The plantation was constantly enlarged, and cash crops of coffee and cocoa were added. The result was that in a poverty-stricken region Oyembo's village was outstandingly prosperous. Then he built one of the best schools for hundreds of miles around, and turned school teacher, not only to children but also to adults.

Shortly after Schweitzer had heard the full story of Oyembo, he was delighted to see him coming up the hill at Lambaréné, and obviously not as a patient.

Schweitzer clasped both hands in his, the two men grinned delightedly at each other, and if there was a wicked twinkle in Oyembo's eyes, Schweitzer had no trouble in forgiving his enjoyment of a good joke on him.

But it would never occur to Schweitzer that the sermons which Oyembo had translated for him, and that his day-to-day contacts with Schweitzer's own way of life at Lambaréné could have had anything to do with Oyembo's subsequent doings.

37

NOTWITHSTANDING Schweitzer's innate modesty, he could not deny what his eyes and his common sense were telling him: that he was gaining ground against the jungle, healing thousands of its sick, and was even freeing some of them from their prisons of darkness and of fear.

Genius in the Jungle

But his overall hope of survival for the hospital was being undermined, not only by his diagnosis of the world's ills but also by the quickening march of events.

For the rainbow that so many had seen over the League of Nations was fading. Stresemann was dead. Briand was dying, and the League of Nations was losing prestige and power. Only the dictator in Italy, the military in Japan, and, most of all, Hitler in Germany were gaining.

General Hindenburg, president of Germany who had promised to protect it from dictatorship, was aging fast and had grown senile. Hitler had run against him for the presidency, and the man who flatly declared that if elected he would become dictator came within four million votes of being elected.

He was gaining power so fast that only a year or two would see him master of Germany.

Meanwhile his agents had wormed themselves into President Hindenburg's household, had gained his confidence, and were whispering to him to face reality and give Hitler the power that would be his anyhow in a short time. As president, they urged, Hindenburg could make Hitler Chancellor, within the framework of legality, and thus save the German people from the blood-bath of a civil war.

It was at this time that Schweitzer received an invitation from the city of Frankfort to deliver an oration there on March 22, 1932, the hundredth anniversary of Goethe's death.

He tried to beg off and sent a cable, suggesting that

there were scholars in Germany more competent than he to deliver the address. The reply to it was courteous but pointed out that since Schweitzer had already accepted the Goethe prize it was only right that he should be the man to speak at the centenary of the great man's death.

It was not only modesty that had prompted Schweitzer to suggest that someone else deliver the address. He had a large library of Goethe material at Lambaréné, and he knew that he could compose a competent enough address for the occasion—if he confined himself to subject matter a hundred years old. The question was, could Schweitzer, who felt so passionately for suffering contemporary humanity, keep silent about the Germany of his day?

He had already written the first and the second of his trilogy on the decay of civilization. But although he had expressed himself simply and in humanly understandable terms, it was still in language of philosophical abstractions that accused no individual in public life, so that even Hitler could read it and feel it had nothing to do with him.

Could Schweitzer content himself with such an address on Goethe, who in his own time had urged that it was every man's duty to fight the evils of his day, even at the risk of life and limb.

Schweitzer sent his acceptance of the invitation to speak at the Goethe centenary.

Africa had again proved too much for Mrs. Schweitzer's health, and she left for Europe before him.

Genius in the Jungle

Schweitzer and four of the hospital nurses sailed for Europe early in 1932.

He wrote the Goethe address aboard ship and finished it just as the *Brazza* steamed into the Gironde River.

In Frankfort the weather on the morning of March 22 was all that one could ask for. There were wreaths at the base of the monument in Goetheplatz, and outside the iron fence that surrounded it men and women stood in silent tribute.

But the main event of the day was in the Opera House, and early in the morning automobiles converged on it, bringing notables not only from all over Germany but from other lands: ambassadors, officials of every rank, men of letters, scientists, august political figures—in all, an illustrious audience.

At a quarter past eleven in the morning, exactly one hundred years after Goethe had drawn his last breath, the opera orchestra played the funeral march from Beethoven's Third Symphony.

When the last note had died away, Schweitzer rose.

To most of his audience it was a time of looming tragedy for Germany. But there were others there, important because of their power, who saw the situation otherwise. They were men for whom the future in Germany held pleasant promise and soaring careers, Hitler's men. They had come to hear Schweitzer, expecting to be favorably impressed; for Hitler, too, claimed Goethe as speaking for him.

Schweitzer's face had the reserve and dignity that

was to be expected in an address on a timeless theme. Most of his speech was scholarly enough to impress everybody and offend no one. His warm personal feeling emerged, for Goethe the man and the genius.

But soon the audience turned tense. Words came that were no longer a century away from the events of the day.

He named no names, nor went into particulars, but the audience knew exactly what he meant when he spoke of "the frightful circumstances of our day. . . . In this most portentous and fateful hour which has ever struck for mankind . . . what is now taking place in this terrible epoch of ours is a gigantic repetition of the drama of Faust . . . with a thousand tongues of flame. . . . In deeds of violence and murder a thousandfold, a brutalized humanity plays its cruel game! Mephistopheles leers at us with a thousand grimaces . . ."

Hitler was within one year of absolute power over Germany, and it took hardihood to say what Schweitzer was saying on so important a rostrum.

Immediately after that Schweitzer gave up his home in Königsfeld, because it was Hitler's Germany. He moved to his home in Günsbach, in French Alsace, and never again set foot in Germany so long as Hitler was in power.

Now history took on a mounting tempo of "frightful circumstance" that more than fulfilled Schweitzer's dark forebodings.

Germany became a vast, terribly efficient prison and torture chamber for all free spirits in the country.

Genius in the Jungle

Many of Schweitzer's illustrious friends were among Hitler's first victims.

Hitler kept his promise to give jobs to German workers. Factories became feverishly busy turning out armaments of war. Nevertheless German workers did not eat much better than before, for the word from on top was, "Guns before butter!"

Hitler increased his army by one hundred thousand every year.

He took Germany out of the League of Nations and was followed by Italy and Japan.

Japan had already begun the conquest of China.

And the Italian dictator began his march of conquest by invading Ethiopia. So that the prelude to the Second World War was already roaring in Africa.

Schweitzer had foreseen much of it, of course, but that made it no easier for him to endure seeing his prophecy come true with such frightening momentum.

All he could do was to prepare Lambaréné, as much as he could, against the inevitable storm, with little reason to think that it would survive. For he knew that this time the war would last longer and that shooting would come closer to Lambaréné than in the First World War.

He raced from country to country, giving recitals, lecturing, accumulating funds against the time when war would stop him.

He pushed himself so unremittingly that a friend protested. "Stop it, you can't burn the candle at both ends!"

Albert Schweitzer

Schweitzer smiled grimly. "Yes, you can, if the candle is long enough."

For the next several years he practically commuted between Europe and Africa in his dual function as doctor to Lambaréné and diagnostician to the world at large.

On January 12, 1939, he left Lambaréné for Europe, planning to stay away some months. But at every port where his ship touched he saw warships gathering. And over the radio in the dining salon Hitler's voice, rasping with blood-lust, broke into every conversation.

By the time Schweitzer had landed at Bordeaux he knew that war was only a matter of months away. He thought it would come in June. Under the circumstances he had to decide where he had to be when war broke out. He felt that his place was with the hundreds of his sick and that he must get back to Lambaréné before war shut off any possibility of return. He left the ship and stayed in Europe twelve days, only long enough to see his wife and his daughter established safely in Switzerland, the only country likely to be above the battle.

Then he went back to Africa.

38

IN SEPTEMBER Hitler let loose his lightning war against Poland. The Second World War was on.

The air over much of the globe resounded with the snarling of dogfights between fleets of planes, and there was the screech of bombs and the ear-splitting counter from the ground.

As the war progressed, nights glared with great fires, city after city, with no letup by day. Barrages of great guns jarred the continents. The seas were churned with explosions and thousands of ships—crews, cargoes and all—finished their voyages in the depths of the ocean.

And the wrong side was winning the war.

When Hitler overran France, Marshal Petain accepted his terms and, with a capital at Vichy, aligned his country with Germany. But under the leadership of General De Gaulle millions of Frenchmen refused to recognize the Vichy government as theirs and fought on the side of the Allies. All French Equatorial Africa —except the Gabon—promptly declared themselves Free French, at war with Hitler.

Albert Schweitzer

In the Gabon, which included the town of Lambaréné, there was conflict. Some Frenchmen felt it would pay them to stay on Hitler's side, and Vichy sent planes and soldiers to support them. Hitler was in need of a base of operations in West Africa, and the Gabon was his best chance to establish it.

Battles broke out between Hitler's collaborationists and the Free French, in the air and on the ground. They raged for two months, during October and November, 1940, and Lambaréné was in the thick of it. Bullets came so near the hospital that Schweitzer put up shields of corrugated iron on the side facing the town.

But even in the heat of battle, both sides came to one agreement.

Schweitzer's hospital was not to be touched.

The result was that although Hitler's ally, Vichy France, had sent a strong fleet of Glenn-Martin planes not a single bomb was aimed at the hospital grounds.

The Free French won, and the hospital took down its corrugated iron shields.

But the *Brazza*, carrying a big consignment of drugs and food for Schweitzer's hospital, was torpedoed, sank to the bottom of the sea and thereby forced a decision on Schweitzer that would have broken the heart of a man much less compassionate than he.

For Hitler's submarines ruled the seas, Lambaréné was cut off from the rest of the world, and Schweitzer would have to carry on indefinitely with what drugs and hospital supplies he had on hand.

Genius in the Jungle

And his stocks were low.

There were more than two hundred natives and whites in the hospital at the time, and, if he kept them on, it meant that his drugs and food would soon give out.

He assembled his sick and put before them the bitter decision he had to make. If he let them all stay, it would not be long before he would have to send them all away. What drugs he had on hand he would have to keep for those whose lives depended on it.

One by one Schweitzer had to decide which man, woman, and child he would have to send away.

There were children who had ailments that were not fatal, but if they were not cured now the youngsters would be crippled for life. There were men and women to whom a few months more at Lambaréné would make the difference between recovery and years of agony. Schweitzer had to close his ears to pleas and cries and, what was hardest of all, he had to bear the silence of many who he knew were in anguish but who took his decision without a murmur.

When it was all over the hospital grounds were almost empty, and for a time there was so little work for Schweitzer to do that he should have been able to relax. But he could still hear the cries of those he had sent away, and could see them limping home along the jungle trails.

Nor was Lambaréné his whole world. Even if he were the kind of man to whom only personal relations mattered, there was his Alsace in the furnace of war and his many friends in Europe to think about, involved in a war he had foreseen. Yet not in his darkest forebodings had he imagined the full extent of its horrors.

But war, serving its own ends, and with the caprice of some mad monster, actually made a contribution to life in West Africa. It needed a military road through the jungles, and from Algiers to Capetown by way of Leopoldville and Brazzaville, and touching Lambaréné, the wilderness for the first time heard the roar of bulldozers, tractors, and other road-making machines that made a great gash along the continent.

They tore through the densest jungle as easily as a plow goes through weeds. They crushed snake nests and armies of traveler ants, and sent beasts of prey stampeding. Now it was the hunters of the jungle who fled, chattering with terror.

Those who manned the machines were granite-faced men to whom the terrors of the jungle were only something they read about for relaxation.

The new road enabled Mrs. Schweitzer to reach Lambaréné three months sooner than it would have taken her otherwise.

Two years later the Schweitzers were also gladdened by the news that their daughter had married M. T. A. Eckert, a Swiss organ builder, and in 1943 they learned that they had a grandchild.

But these windfalls of personal happiness came against a background of a world shuddering with war—and such a war! Schweitzer, to whom science was a healer, had to face the fact that Satanic uses were being made of it, most of all by Hitler's scientists, with human life as the cheapest and most expendable of materials. Even then there was such a glut of it, from the Nazi, Italian, and Japanese point of view, that their leaders had chosen men and women to whom torture and killing was food and drink, and had put them in positions of power over millions of the expendables. They were made the chiefs of concentration camps, gas chambers, and incinerators. Six and a half million Jews alone were thus disposed of. In their orgies these overseers took moving pictures and still photographs. Later, when the Allies had captured these pictures and showed them to the world, men and women averted their eyes or literally turned sick at the sight.

As to Hitler, Mussolini, Tojo, and their associates—malignant as cancer and revolting as dysentery—they yet managed by their innate and incredible vulgarity of nature to rob even death of some of its dignity.

And they were winning the war.

With the victory of the Free French in Equatorial Africa the shooting there had stopped. But the strain and drain on the hospital at Lambaréné kept mounting.

European women whose husbands had been called to war dared not stay on alone in isolated jungle regions, and Schweitzer could not very well refuse to give them shelter. Other Europeans, who were unable to get away and had fallen sick, also had to be taken in. And there were always the natives whom their medicine men had rejected as incurable but whom Schweitzer could not turn away.

Some of the hospital doctors and nurses had fallen ill and had to be sent away to recuperate. Others were drafted for service on the firing lines.

The situation bore down so heavily on the Schweitzers and their few remaining helpers that he was moved to write: "We had to draw on our last reserves in order to meet the demands of the hospital. Not to fall ill—to keep fit for work—this was our constant daily care. . . . Not one of us must collapse, for there could be no replacements for a long time. . . . So we carried on."

His more personal dream he expressed in a letter to a friend. "Oh, for one free day when I could sleep long enough to get rid of the fatigue that invades me more and more; to concentrate on finishing my book; to study my music and play the organ at leisure; to talk, to dream, to read for pure refreshment. . . . When will that day come? Will it ever come?"

In spite of Hitler's submarines, help for Lambaréné began to filter through, from England, Switzerland, and, most of all, from America. American promises of help came in a letter asking what Schweitzer needed. With a sort of wishful thinking he wrote out a full list of the hospital's needs. America promptly dispatched the shipment he had asked for. But it took more than a year for it to reach Lambaréné.

But when it did arrive there were cries of joy as each box and crate was opened. Schweitzer's surgical gloves, for instance, had been too small for him. "Now what an immense relief it is to have gloves at last that do not torment me!" Those in charge of the kitchen rejoiced over new cooking utensils. "For the first time since the Hospital was founded we had large thermos bottles for the ice we get in the village." Spectacles arrived that enabled whites and natives to do their work for the first time.

On Schweitzer's seventieth birthday, January 14, 1945, London was still under the deluge of Hitler's latest scientific triumphs, the V-1 and V-2 rockets. But a cable came to Lambaréné that the British Broadcasting Corporation, a government agency, would tell the world about Schweitzer that day.

One of the patients had a portable radio, and a graphic picture of the reception of the broadcast is given in Hermann Hagedorn's *Prophet in the Wilderness*.

"All the white patients and the hospital staff were gathered about Schweitzer and his wife that evening to listen to England's tribute. The wind, gently swaying the palm fronds outside the open window, brought no relief indoors from the stifling heat. The lights of the radio went on, but for a minute the listening ears heard only the chirping of the crickets and, from across the river, the beat of a tom-tom. Suddenly, crystal clear, the voice of the theologian, Nathaniel Micklem, came from the loudspeaker, telling the story of Albert Schweitzer. One of Schweitzer's own organ recordings followed, as clear of atmospheric intrusion, as intimate and persuasive as though the listeners were in the nave of the great Abbey and Schweitzer were actually at the keyboard. The announcer said: 'Dr. Schweitzer is listening at this moment in Lambaréné.' And space was nothing and they seemed all together—his friends in the London studio, he and his wife and friends in the heart of Africa, and the listeners throughout the world."

Meanwhile the tide of war had been turning at last against Hitler, Mussolini, and Japan. The Russians had taken their stand at Stalingrad. The underground movements of resistance in the invaded countries in Europe, aided by the Allies, were gaining in destructiveness. Allied armies, too, especially America's millions of men and women on the ground, on the seas, and in the air, were taking the offensive. In the Pacific the Allies were nearing Japan, island by island. And the greatest productive machinery the world had ever seen, America's "arsenal of democracy," was increasing at a time when the enemies' factories and cities were being shattered. Hitler, Mussolini, and Tojo were now reaping the harvest they had sown.

Italy was the first to be crushed, and Mussolini, who wanted to "cut a gash in history with a lion's paw," was strung up by his heels, dead and dishonored. In Berlin, in a luxurious underground bombproof shelter, Hitler, the Goebbels family, and others of the Nazi chiefs met grisly deaths.

At midday on Monday May 7, 1945, Schweitzer was sitting at his writing table finishing some urgent letters which had to catch the river boat by two o'clock that afternoon. A patient who had a portable radio came to Schweitzer's window and called out that according to a German report, relayed from the radio station at Leopoldville, in the Belgian Congo, Germany would surrender unconditionally.

Schweitzer listened to him and hesitated. He wanted badly to drop everything and open his heart to the hour. He knew that over most of the world, except in Asia, where the war was still on, millions of men, women, and children could draw a free breath now for the time being. They would sleep that night. Everywhere people were cheering, dancing, and weeping with joy. Many were on their knees in thanksgiving. Dazed and tired soldiers, sailors, fliers, and other combatants were getting drunk or staring stupefied at the sky, knowing there was no longer danger there.

But those letters *were* urgent, and they did have to catch the two o'clock boat. So Schweitzer went on writing.

Then there were heart cases at the hospital that worried him, and he went to see them. There were still other patients who took up more of his time.

It was only late in the afternoon that he ordered the big summoning bell to be rung, and when everybody was gathered he told them what they already knew, but they had been waiting for him to speak for them.

He made a brief announcement, because he was too worn out to make a speech. Besides, the plantation needed his immediate attention, and exhausted as he was he went there to do what was needed.

Albert Schweitzer

Late that evening, when he was finally alone, he allowed himself "to think and try to imagine the meaning of the end of the hostilities and what innumerable people must be feeling on this night."

Then he took down a book from the shelf, the sayings of the ancient Chinese sage, Lao-tse, and read: "Weapons are disastrous implements, no tools for a noble being. . . . Quiet and peace are for him the highest good. . . ."

But man had still an explosion in the making, the greatest of them all. He had learned to split the atom, and over two Japanese cities a bomb apiece fell. Their effects frightened even the victors. It was a question even in the minds of those most qualified to judge, atomic scientists, whether man had not invented something that might blow up the whole globe into a drift of radioactive dust. But for some twelve million men, women, and children, who had experienced the war, it was only an academic question. They were already dust.

But on Tuesday, August 4th of the same year, Lambaréné heard that Japan, too, had surrendered and that the Allies had won.

39

VICTORY did not ease conditions for Schweitzer and his hospital. The food situation had been bad in the Gabon since 1945. Rain had fallen in the dry season of that year, preventing the natives from growing a crop of two staples, bananas and tapioca. This meant that food was also running short at the hospital. The Mission schools at Lambaréné had closed for lack of food, and there was the likelihood that, after all he had gone through, Schweitzer would have to close the hospital for the same reason.

Fortunately a farseeing District Officer at Tschibanga had insisted on rice cultivation in his region, and some of it helped Schweitzer save his hospital. Nevertheless he was so pessimistic that he wrote: "The continued existence of the Hospital in the future will prove very difficult. We might indeed entertain whether it will be possible at all when we consider the widespread and as yet incalculable impoverishment in every direction."

It was not only the mood of a very tired man, who had been in Africa too long at a time and overworking.

Albert Schweitzer

He was looking ahead and seeing a humanity that would have to pay for two world wars.

But it was not like him to end on a note of defeat. "Nevertheless," he went on, "we are confident that the friends of Lambaréné will remain faithful to it even in the difficult circumstances that are before us."

His confidence proved justified, and the reports of the hospital, as brought back by some American friends who visited it in the summer of 1947, showed a relatively peaceful and prosperous picture.

It had beds for three hundred fifty patients. There was an ample staff of doctors, nurses, orderlies, and other workers. There were a score and more of native youngsters who had been born at the hospital and were being brought up there.

The plantation was now supplying fresh fruit not only for the hospital but for its neighbors. At the staff table there were big bowls of fruit salads, of oranges, tangerines, pineapples, and grapefruit, and diners were urged to take several helpings.

On Sundays the river at the hospital resounded with the chant of native visitors as they paddled their dugouts:

"Tzeh, poba-poba, tzeh, tzut-tzut; tzeh, poba-poba, tzeh, tzut-tzut."

There was so much traffic to and from the hospital that some of the dugouts were doing a lively taxi business.

Schweitzer had time to play a little with his pets, of which there was a veritable menagerie. There were

Genius in the Jungle

baby antelopes who nudged him for attention and lived in the same room with the zinc-lined piano, which Schweitzer now found time to play.

All over the hospital grounds geese, hens, turkeys, African sheep, monkeys, dogs, and cats wandered about at will. There was even a rugged old pelican. At six in the evening, which it had decided was closing hour for Schweitzer's living quarters—except for Schweitzer—it took up its roost on a beam overhead, and anyone who ventured there after hours risked a crack on the head from the pelican's big bill. The bird has become so publicized that it is probably the most famous pelican in the world.

Meals for the hospital were prepared under the care of a Swiss dietician.

Perhaps the one sinister note was the heavy wooden bars that were nailed across every window. It was a reminder that the jungle and its wild life were only yards away. One night, for instance, after Schweitzer had retired he heard a soft scuffle outside his window. He went over and found himself gazing into the eyes of a full-grown panther.

The following year, after nearly ten years of Africa without a vacation, Schweitzer went back to Europe. His wife, because of ill health, had had to leave sooner. As usual, Schweitzer arrived in Europe in a state of exhaustion.

He went first to Günsbach, and found that he had chosen the site of his guest house wisely. It had survived the artillery fire of the Second World War, as had the village itself.

He and his wife had to have mountain air, however. and now that Germany was free of Hitler the Schweitzers went back to their beloved Königsfeld. The family reunion there included four grandchildren Schweitzer saw for the first time.

40

FOR years Schweitzer's friends in America had been urging him to come for a visit. Harvard University had invited him to deliver the Lowell Lectures and be an honored guest at the Tercentenary Celebration of its founding. Dr. Albert Einstein, at that time head of the Institute for Advanced Studies at Princeton, had invited him to come there and use its facilities to finish his third volume on the philosophy ot civilizanon. "There, in this sorry world of ours," he said of Schweitzer, "is a great man."

Genius in the Jungle

But Schweitzer had been afraid to come here. Gandhi, the spiritual leader and martyr of India, had also been asked to visit America but had refused. He had felt that the richest land in the world was too materialistic to understand his emphasis on the spiritual. Schweitzer had the same misgivings.

But in the summer of 1949, the two hundredth anniversary of the birth of Goethe was to be celebrated, among other places, at Aspen, Colorado, under the auspices of some of the most celebrated educators, artists, and humanitarians. Schweitzer was invited to deliver an address on Goethe.

His wife and his daughter had already visited America, and their reports must have been a factor in his acceptance.

American reporters and cameramen are no respectors of persons apart from their intrinsic worth. When the queen of a European country, for instance, arrived here some years ago, a ship news cameraman called, "Hey, Queen, park the body a little to the left, will ya?" His words caused amusement in America but no particular shock, partly because the woman expected everybody to kneel before her.

When Schweitzer arrived there was more than the usual turnout of ship news reporters, photographers, and newsreel men. They swarmed about him, to the astonishment of many of his fellow passengers, who had not known he was on board or had never heard of him. Hardened newsmen reported that almost never before had a visiting celebrity been treated by reporters and photographers with the respect, verging on awe, they accorded Schweitzer.

And the press all over America treated him the same way. One reporter wrote of America's chance to "touch the hem of the man's garment."

Even "the man on the street" began to hear of him.

Schweitzer found that America understood him very well indeed.

He in turn was touched, for instance, when someone told him of the heavy winter storms of 1948-49 that would have killed hundreds of thousands of cattle more than it did in our West had it not been for the food that had been dropped to them from planes. "Ah," Schweitzer said with tears in his eyes, "what a magnificent achievement! *Vive L'Amerique!*"

And Americans have responded, with more than words, by *their* wish for long life to Albert Schweitzer and his works.

Long ago someone asked him why he never took in the sights in the cities and countries where he gave lectures and concerts. He smiled. "I'll begin sightseeing when I am seventy-five."

He did not stop for sightseeing in America. Within a few months of his seventy-fifth birthday, he was hurrying back to the Gabon, heartened by the material and other aid he had received for the big colony of lepers he had established there.

"How wonderful have been the experiences vouchsafed me all these years!" he has written. "When I first went to Africa I prepared to make three sacrifices. To abandon the organ, to renounce the academic teaching activities, to which I had given my heart, and to lose my financial independence, relying for the rest of life on the help of friends.

"These three sacrifices I had begun to make, and only my intimate friends knew what they cost me.

"But now there has happened to me what happened to Abraham when he was prepared to sacrifice his son. I, like him, have been spared the sacrifice."

Publisher's Postscript

On the morning of Sunday, September 5, 1965, the world was saddened to learn that Albert Schweitzer had died the previous night. The great humanitarian, theologian, musician, and physician—but always preeminently the humanitarian—was ninety years old and for some days his strength had been ebbing.

Few men have been honored in their own lifetimes as Dr. Schweitzer was honored; fewer still have deserved such homage. His work in his hospital at Lambaréné meant everything to him—so much so that when he was granted the Nobel Peace Prize in 1952, he could not find the time to go to Oslo to receive the $33,000 award until two years later. And then he gave the money to the hospital.

Dr. Schweitzer was buried near his jungle hospital in a plain wooden coffin. The simple funeral service was read by Dr. Walter Munz, a young Swiss physician. Native women chanted:

"Laonni inani kende kende." (May you rest in peace.)

Tributes to the fallen leader were paid by great personages all over the globe. President Johnson said:

"The world has lost a truly universal figure. His message and his example, which have lightened the darkest years of this century, will continue to strengthen all those who strive to create a world living in peace and brotherhood."

Queen Elizabeth II of Great Britain wrote: "His great work in so many fields will long be remembered and his humanity will inspire this and future generations."

The preceding paragraphs were not written by Joseph Gollomb, the author of this book. It would have been appropriate had he lived to pay a final tribute to the man of whom he wrote so lovingly, but this was not to be.